How to Write a
Narrative Investigation Report

A Monograph In

THE POLICE SCIENCE SERIES

Edited by

V. A. LEONARD
Professor Emeritus of Police Administration
Department of Police Science and Administration
Washington State University
Pullman, Washington

How to Write
a
Narrative Investigation
Report

By

WILLIAM DIENSTEIN

Professor of Social Science and Criminology
Fresno State College
Fresno, California

Second Printing

Police Science Series

CHARLES C THOMAS • PUBLISHER
Springfield • Illinois • U.S.A.

Published and Distributed Throughout the World by

CHARLES C THOMAS • PUBLISHER

Bannerstone House

301-327 East Lawrence Avenue, Springfield, Illinois, U.S.A.

Natchez Plantation House

735 North Atlantic Boulevard, Fort Lauderdale, Florida, U.S.A.

First Printing, 1964
Second Printing, 1969

With THOMAS BOOKS *careful attention is given to all details of manufacturing and design. It is the Publisher's desire to present books that are satisfactory as to their physical qualities and artistic possibilities and appropriate for their particular use.* THOMAS BOOKS *will be true to those laws of quality that assure a good name and good will*

Printed in the United States of America

N-1

FOREWORD

Narrative report writing is a skill and an art. There are no short-cuts to good report writing. Good report writing requires training and practice. It is hoped that this book will assist those who strive to improve their ability to communicate.

ACKNOWLEDGMENTS

THE WRITER wishes to express his appreciation for the assistance and cooperation of the following persons in the preparation of this book:

Richard C. Steinmetz, Chief Special Agent, Mutual Investigation Bureau, Chicago, Illinois;

Bradford M. Crittenden, Commissioner, California Highway Patrol, Sacramento, California;

Inspector D. T. Donaldson, Commander, Training Division, California Highway Patrol;

Melvin A. Willmirth, Sheriff, Fresno County, Fresno, California;

Robert L. Saum, Patrol Captain, Fresno County Sheriff's Office, Fresno, California;

Arnold P. Biella, Ph.D., Dean, Department of Humanities, Alameda State College, Hayward, California;

Miss Dorothy E. Smith, Associate Professor of English, Fresno State College, Fresno, California;

Mrs. Wilma F. Wight, Associate Professor of Secretarial Administration, Fresno State College, Fresno, California;

Mrs. Harold Schlintz, Fresno, California.

WILLIAM DIENSTEIN

CONTENTS

How to Write a
Narrative Investigation Report

INTRODUCTION

WHY SHOULD REPORTS BE WRITTEN?

THE LAW ENFORCEMENT officer writes an investigation report to record his activities and findings. The report is the written recollection of the officer and provides a permanent official record of his actions, his observations, and his discoveries. The report is the written record of the impressions upon the writer of the circumstances of a situation. The investigation report is the word picture of an investigation, beginning with a complaint, order, offense, or arrest. It is the permanent record of the case, the basic reference to the case, the basis for evaluation of what has been done, the basis for deciding further action, and the basis for prosecution. In fact, the report becomes "the case."

The report is the method by which an officer communicates his findings to those interested in his activities. Although reporting may be done orally to colleagues or immediate superiors, a written report, as stated above, is a permanent reference and record. There can be no doubt as to what the officer reported. The written report enables a fellow officer to know what another officer has done and found. It enables the superior officer to know what his men have done; it enables him to keep track of the various activities and investigations of his men; it enables him to know the types of crimes being committed and the manner in which they are committed; it enables him to see relationships among the findings of his men from which he may be able to determine possible connections among cases. The written report is the basis upon which the superior officer can offer advice and make suggestions for further investigation or subsequent handling of the case. Finally, it is the record upon which the office of the prosecutor bases its action.

Information obtained from the various reports of a police

3

department can be tabulated by a central office within the department to give a complete crime picture of a city or of an area within the city. Reports aid in the deployment of men and equipment in keeping with the crime picture at a given time. Men can be concentrated in areas showing a rise in particular types of offenses. Men can be alerted to be on the lookout for signs of the known *modus operandi* of the unidentified perpetrators of a series of offenses.

The records of a police department based upon the reports of its personnel are an aid in the planning of the police budget and the distribution of funds within a department. Long range planning for the department to meet changing crime conditions is based on the information from reports.

Reports can be used to point up the training needs of personnel so that they may be better able to cope with specific crime conditions. The weaknesses and strengths of the department can be ascertained and training programs developed to eliminate the weaknesses.

The report serves as a record for later reference. A single report may be only one part of a more complex case on which other officers within the department as well as officers of other agencies within the state or in other states may be working. The activities and findings of any one officer in such a case may have unforeseen implications and ramifications, and his reports may be of inestimable value to other officers and agencies. His report may form the basis for plans and actions by personnel and agencies of whom he may be unaware.

The report represents a convenient method for keeping other interested local public agencies such as the fire, health, welfare, probation, and parole departments informed of conditions with which they are concerned. Since the welfare of the community is the concern of all, especially of public agencies, and crime is an offense against the community, the work of the police agency in combatting offenses against the community should be available to assist other public agencies when appropriate.

In addition to aiding the work of other public departments and thereby developing the cooperation that is so essential to local government, the information derived from reports can be used to keep the public informed of police problems and accomplishments. Such information becomes the basis for public support of the police agency. Reports then become a foundation for a public relations program acquainting the community with the activities of its law enforcement agency.

If the investigation report goes to the office of the prosecutor, he will be dependent on the facts set out in the report in determining whether or not he has sufficient evidence for a prosecution. If he decides to prosecute, he must rely on the report to show (1) that an offense was committed; (2) who perpetrated the offense; (3) who was the victim; (4) what evidence is available for presentation; (5) what witnesses should be subpoenaed; (6) what the defense might be; and (7) what strategy he should use to counteract it.

From the foregoing, it can be seen that the quality of the investigation reports and police records have a direct relationship to the efficiency of a police department and to the administration of justice in a community. It cannot be overemphasized that an investigation, no matter how well done, can be no better than the manner in which the report is written. The investigator must remember that his report tells the reader the manner in which the investigation was conducted, and is the basis for evaluation of the quality of the investigation. A poor report of a good investigation will give the impression of a poor investigation.

WHEN SHOULD REPORTS BE WRITTEN

Reports are sources of information. Reports should be written whenever department policy prescribes that they be written. For example, a department may require that a report be completed at the conclusion of each tour of duty on the condition of the vehicle used. It may require a "contact" report which includes the names, locations, and reasons for stopping and questioning any person. The number of report forms will vary from department to department. Usually, the number of report forms in any police department is related to the kinds of records the department maintains.

Many police officers "fight" reports. The result is that they make their job more difficult and less pleasant. If the officer will take the time to discover the "why" of the report, he may find his task easier. For example, the vehicle report mentioned above is important to the maintenance division of any department. A poorly operating vehicle is no asset to a police officer.

In general, reports may be classified into four large categories: complaint, offense, arrest, and investigation. A complaint report is completed for every communication to the police department requesting police action. An offense report is completed for every incident or occurrence requiring official police action. An arrest report is completed for every person taken into custody. An investigation report is written by every officer assigned to a case and by each officer who has information about a case even though he may not be assigned to the case.

From another viewpoint, it may be said that reports should be written whenever the action taken and the findings made could be used in the future. This may seem to be a large order. Certainly, not all actions, contacts, observations, and the like will require official department reports. But the officer may want to have written notation of many of his actions, contacts, observations, etc. which he suspects may have consequences. He therefore maintains a personal notebook in which he keeps such information as he deems essential to his work. His notebooks should be filed by dates. He may maintain a name file with cross reference to the notebook entry by date. The value of a personal notebook is as great as the ingenuity of the officer.

For example, while on patrol in a sparsely populated suburban area, an officer noticed a car, which did not seem to belong, parked in the driveway of one of the luxurious houses. The car was not in keeping with the economic status of the neighborhood or with the occupants' friends. The officer jotted down a description of the car, license number, make, model, color, etc., in his notebook, noting the time and date. He habitually recorded in this notebook any unusual events, calls answered, and people contacted. A few days later his office received a report of a burglary from the occupants of the house in whose driveway the officer had noted the strange car. They had been away for several days, and on returning to their residence discovered the burglary. Since the burglary occurred in his territory, the officer refreshed his memory with his notebook and reported the information he had noted about the vehicle. When the investigators checked out the information, they found the loot, the burglar, and loot from numerous other burglaries.

However, it is not the purpose of this monograph to discuss in detail the policeman's notebook and the many report forms used in police departments. There are several good books which perform this task. (See Reference List.) Our primary concern is with the narrative aspects of report writing, that is, the telling about activities, observations, findings in such a way as to communicate information effectively. Most department forms require either the checking of listed items or the filling-in of specifically required information such as name, address, date, victim, etc. Usually there is a space for "remarks." It is in the "remarks" section of the various reports that the officer will narrate such information as he deems necessary to complete the story the report is designed to convey.

It might be well at this point to distinguish between a report and a record. A report may become a record, but not all records are reports. A record may refer to a report since the report is the source of the record. The report is the handiwork of the officer. The record is the handiwork of others who take specific information from the report and transcribe it upon the appropriate record form. The record stores the particular bits of information appearing in the report in various classifications or categories. Information from a single report may be transcribed to several record forms. For example, the information from an arrest report may be distributed to records maintained in the following files: name, alias, location, offense, property, *modus operandi,* time, etc.

The records division of a police department, whether it be large or small, is the permanent memory center of the accumulated activities of the personnel of that department. Its advantage lies in the fact that it does not depend upon the vagaries of an individual's recollection and that it outlives any individual. Personnel come and go, but the records division continues to accumulate and store information of the department's activity. Too often, the importance of records is not recognized, and as a consequence, records are not utilized fully or adequately. It is well to remember the records in a record division are no more accurate than the reporting of the police personnel.

2

WHAT INFORMATION IS INCLUDED IN A REPORT?

W HAT IS INCLUDED in a report depends upon the purpose of the report. The purpose of the report is to inform the reader of certain activities and the outcome of these activities. In an investigation, the object is to secure the information which explains an occurrence. Therefore, in writing an investigation report the officer should always bear in mind that the primary purpose of his writing is to inform. He is trying to tell his problem and his actions as they relate to that problem to the reader of the report. In preparing his narration, he cannot assume that the reader will have any knowledge about the case. He cannot expect the reader to fill in any details. His only assumption can be that the reader's only information about the investigation will come from the report.

The content pattern or content outline of a report should include answers to five basic questions which, although familiar to peace officers, are so obvious as to be overlooked. These five questions are

1. WHO is involved?
2. WHAT happened?
3. WHEN did it happen?
4. WHERE did it happen?
5. HOW did it happen?

Unless these five questions are answered in the final report of any investigation, there is no case. The answers to these questions constitute the elements of the case. The answers constitute the basis for further action on the case. If the answers are incomplete, or if one or more of the five questions are not answered adequately or are omitted, further investigation is necessary. Unless the answers to these five questions are evident and complete, the report cannot be used as a basis for further action.

The word WHY has been omitted from the questions that must be answered in a report. The reason for the omission is based upon the meaning and implication given to the word. WHY, when applied to human action, refers to motivation. Motivation refers to the initiating impulse or drive to the action that resulted in a particular outcome. Human personality is so constituted that most people when asked for a reason for action, for the WHY of a particular behavior, will come up with an *answer*. However, the answer may not coinside with the real reason or the real motivant. Many times we don't like to admit that we don't really know why we did a particular thing. So we usually attribute to ourselves a motive or reason that appears logical to us.

When we seek to explain the WHY of an occurrence, we lead ourselves into speculation without being fully aware that we are speculating. Such behavior may lead us astray. Since we tend to project onto others our logic, we forget that our logic may not be the logic of another. The way we think is determined by a multitude of factors which is unique to each of us. To say that we would do thus and so under a particular set of conditions may be a guess; to say that if we were so and so we would do thus and so under the same set of conditions may be fiction. Yet, too often, we fall into this trap, and our activities are guided into those channels that tend to support our logic rather than into all the channels that may give us some information that can be verified. In short, in attempting to answer the question WHY, the investigation may be channeled into so limited an area that it becomes a false trail. The only verification of a motive is the word of the perpetrator, and as indicated, he may not be aware what the motive really is.

Let us now attempt to indicate what constitutes a complete answer to each of the WHO, WHAT, WHEN, WHERE, and HOW questions.[1]

[1]I keep six honest serving men
    they taught me all I knew;
Their names are What and Why and When
    and How and Where and Who.

Rudyard Kipling: "The Elephant's Child,"
Bartlett's *Quotations,* Little Brown & Company (New York, 1948) p. 784.

WHO IS INVOLVED?

Who is the victim?
Who is the suspect?
Who is a witness?
Who reported the case?

Who is involved? covers all the persons that are discovered to be connected in any way with the occurrence under investigation. In reporting who is involved, each individual is identified separately in such a manner that he cannot be confused with any other individual. This identification is accomplished through a complete personal description obtained from such sources as records, photographs, witnesses, and observation. Most police agencies suggest a listing similar to the following which indicates the items that make up a complete personal description. All of the following items may not be completed by the investigator until the conclusion of the investigation. Moreover, it may not be necessary to complete all of them, but knowing these items may prevent the investigator from overlooking important aspects of information vital to answering the question, "Who is involved?"

1. Name: In full, no initials unless they are the name.
2. Aliases: All known names used with various spellings; nicknames are included as well as variations on the real name.
3. Addresses: Include present and all past addresses known with approximate dates of residence. Use street, number, apartment number, name of apartment house, city, postal zone, and state.
4. Sex: Male or female.
5. Race (skin color): White, black, yellow, red, brown.
6. Nationality: Country of origin; if naturalized, date and place of naturalization.
7. Occupation: List all jobs at which person has worked. Indicate primary job.
8. Age: If exact age is known, give it with birthdate and birthplace. If unknown, estimate age in multiples of five and so indicate.
9. Marital Status: Single, married, divorced, separated, an-

nulled, widowed; maiden name of spouse or ex-spouse; date and place of marriage, divorce, separation, annulment or widowhood; all known addresses of spouse and ex-spouses.

10. Service in Armed Forces: Dates of service, rank, serial number, branch of service, job or specialty assignment, identification of assignment and units. If in service, include name of most recent commanding officer.

11. Physical Description: Any information that identifies the subject as an individual and sets him apart from all others as well as the following:

    Height: if estimate, so indicate; arrive at estimate by comparison with a known height.

    Weight: if estimate, so indicate; arrive at estimate by comparison with a known weight.

    Build: stocky, large, heavy, stout or very stout; average, medium; thin, slender, slight; muscular, well developed, poorly developed.

    Posture: normal, erect, stooped, head forward, hunched.

    Complexion: florid, ruddy, sallow, pale; fair, dark; clear, blotched, marked, pimply, freckled.

    Hair: color; thick or thin; curly, wavy; cut, part, style; front, back, complete, baldness; note possibility of a wig.

    Forehead: high, low; bulging, receding; wide, narrow.

    Eyes: color of iris; size—large, small; any peculiarities —protruding, sunken, pouches; glasses—type worn, description.

    Eyebrows: slant—up or down; bushy, sparse, plucked; arched, wavy, horizontal, connected; texture— heavy, thin, short hair, long hair, penciled.

    Nose: large, small; pug, hooked, straight, flat, broken; skewed right or left; upturned, downturned; nostrils —large or small; hairy or clean.

    Moustache: color, size, shape; short, stubby, long; pointed ends, turned-up ends, drooping ends; trimmed, line, thick.

Whiskers: color, size, shape; Van Dyke, straight, rounded, goatee, side, muttonchops. If subject is smooth shaven, has he ever worn whiskers or moustache.

Mouth: large, small; drooping or upturned corners; open, crooked, distorted during speech or laughter; wide, narrow; thin line.

Lips: thick, thin, puffy; drooping lower; upturned upper; protruding; short; harelip.

Teeth: large, small; prominent, projecting; even, uneven; color; fillings; missing; false; broken; gold; conspicuous dental work.

Ears: small, large; close to head, projecting from head; pierced; lobes attached, lobes dangling; cauliflower.

Chin: small, large; square, pointed, round; double; dimpled; jutting, receding, flat, cleft.

Face: long, round, square, peg top; fat, thin; sunken cheeks; high cheekbones, prominent cheekbones; pockmarked, freckles, blemishes, moles; puffy.

Neck: long, short; thick, thin, puffed; folds in back; bull; prominent Adam's apple.

Shoulders: broad, narrow; square, round, sloping; one lower.

Stomach: flat, prominent; firm, soft, bulging.

Hands: large, small; fingers—long, short, missing, stains, marks, stubby, wide with rounded tips; peculiarity of skin.

Arms: long, short; heavy, muscular, thin; hairy, clean; freckled.

Fingernails: short, long, broken, bitten off; dirty, manicured, well-kept, trimmed, polished—color.

Visible Marks When Fully Clothed: scars, blemishes, peculiarities.

Walk: slow, fast; long, short strides; lumbering, spritely, shuffling, bouncy, loping gait.

Dress: neat, slovenly; conservative, loud; type—work clothes, business, sport; cheap, expensive; unmatched; headgear type, description; shoes, description; affinity to particular colors.

Jewelry: kind, where worn.

Speech: slow, rapid; clear, mumbling; impediment; accent; effeminate, masculine; falsetto; rasping, loud, soft; habitual expressions; peculiarities of grammar or pronounciation.

Blemishes: describe and locate; moles, warts, birthmarks, scars, scratches, tatoo marks; etc.

Habits: clean, dirty; fastidious, sloppy; chews (what and brand name); smokes (what and brand name); addict (kind); gambler (kind); frequenter of pool parlors, bowling alleys, dance halls, taverns, night clubs, athletic events, resorts, movies; favorite actor, actress; favorite type of movie, TV, or radio programs; etc.

Disease: any chronic ailment; tuberculosis; ulcers; diabetes; asthma; venereal; etc.

Disabilities: lameness, stiffness, broken members improperly healed; deafness, poor vision; loss of members; etc.

Pastime: recreational activities, hobbies (see habits).

Peculiarities: those characteristics not mentioned elsewhere that definitely differentiate and set apart the subject from others; twitching of features; sexual or moral pervert; bad table manners; attitude toward foods; never wears a hat; always wears a particular type of hat; clicks teeth while talking: smacks or licks lips; use of hands when sitting or talking; kind of laugh; clearing of throat, sniffling, coughing; poker face, shifty-eyed; kind of automobile driver; extrovert, introvert; bow legs, pigeon toed, knock-kneed; etc.

12. Relatives: Names and addresses, occupations; degree of relationship—close, frequent; etc.

13. Associates: Male and female; names and addresses; occupations; those who would be likely to know of subject's movements or whereabouts and with whom he is likely to communicate.

14. Organization Membership: Fraternal, political, social, trade, professional, etc.

15. Photographs: Obtain photographs and any other representations of the person, be they paintings, sketches, or caricatures; approximate date of representation should be obtained.

16. Fingerprint Record.

The above items apply to all persons implicated in an investigation. Even the physical description of a victim may be important in that an offender may select certain physical types as victims. In certain cases it may be advisable to have physical descriptions of witnesses.

Example: A witness may habitually wear glasses, but at the time of witnessing an occurrence be without his glasses. This could be very significant, since without glasses the witness may not have been able to see what he described.

Example: A witness claims not to have heard a sound which is an essential element in an occurrence. It could be that the witness was hard of hearing and usually wore a hearing aid, but at the time of the occurrence had it turned down or off or wasn't wearing it.

When reporting a person's description, it should be set out in tabular form, each characteristic in a separate paragraph, to make for easy reading. The description is adequate when whoever reads it can identify the person described in any group of people.

The investigating officer must remember that it is easier to discard information than it is to obtain it after the initial opportunity has passed. At the beginning of an investigation the officer does not know what bit of information is going to be essential. A general rule is to get all the information one can while the opportunity presents itself.

WHAT HAPPENED?

What took place?
What offense was committed?
What are the elements of the offense?
What was the object of the attack?

What Happened? tells about the occurrence. Be specific, be precise, be accurate. In describing what happened the investigator must stick to the observable facts and to the statements of wit-

nesses. The description of what happened—the occurrence—
should identify the offense. The identification of the offense
should be as specific as possible: burglary, robbery, rape, murder,
assault, battery, worthless checks, arson, counterfeiting, extortion,
threats, peeping Tom, prowler, theft—from auto, from person,
from whatever source, by trick, by device, shoplifting, auto theft,
etc.

Any offense consists of a number of elements. These elements must be shown in order to establish the offense. The elements of an offense are stated in the description of the offense as
it appears in the penal code.

If the case involves a theft of any type, indicate specifically
what was taken. Give the general class of the articles taken:
money, clothing, jewelry, silverware, etc. Then name, describe,
and give the value of the articles.

As an aid in the description of property, the following points
may be used as a guide:

1. Name of Article: Every article has a name. Be exact. Give the
   general classification and the specific designation.
   Example: Watch, wrist, trade name
2. Material From Which Made: Every article is made of some
   substance. Identify the substance or combination of sub-
   stances. If you can't, then guess and say it is a guess or
   "looks like."
3. Serial Numbers: Serial numbers are generally used by manu-
   facturers to identify the product as to its place in sequence
   of production. Learn which articles carry numbers and
   where.
4. Monograms and Inscriptions: Articles of apparel and jewelry
   among others may contain inscriptions of various types.
   Write in quotation marks exact initials, dates, and inscriptions that appear on the article; give exact location of in-
   scription.
5. Manufacturer's, Retailer's, or Trade Names: Many articles are
   identified with names of various types that appear on
   labels attached to the article, are impressed upon the
   article, or are a part of the article.
6. Model Numbers: Various articles are identified with a model
   numbering system.

7. Size: All articles have size. The adjectives may vary from the very specific to the very general.

8. Color: All articles have color either solid or in combination. Specify the various colors of the various parts.

9. Shape: All articles have shape. Describe the shape or draw a sketch of the shape.

10. Marks of Identification: Articles that have been in use carry with them special marks of that use. Clothing may have laundry or dry cleaning marks, wear marks, soil marks, alterations, repair marks, burn holes, mismatched buttons, etc. Also owners sometimes put marks on tools, labels on clothing and the like for identification purposes.

11. Age and Condition: The age of an article is determined by date of purchase when known. The appearance of the article may be described as new, slightly used, evidence of considerable use, as well as the kind of treatment to which it was subjected. The general condition of any article may be almost new, almost worn out, in good operating condition, in poor operating condition.

12. Value of Article: Articles have monetary value. Usually the value would be the purchase price or replacement price. (Insurance companies may depreciate for use, but that is another problem.)

In summary, the purpose of any description is that another person may identify the object on the basis of that description. Many law enforcement agencies have manuals which set out in great detail how to describe specific articles. Investigators must utilize information available from dealers and business men for describing and identifying articles.

WHEN DID IT HAPPEN?

When in time did the occurrence take place?
At what hour?
On what day?
In what month?
In what year?
Was it day or night?
Was it clear or cloudy?
Was it foggy, misty, raining, smoggy, snowing, hailing, sleeting, etc?

When did it happen? attempts to fix the time of the occurrence. If the exact time of the happening cannot be fixed, then approximate the time on the basis of available evidence. Such approximations should be labeled as approximations and should be set out as inclusive periods. Set the time of day between possible limits within a single day or between certain hours of one day and a subsequent day.

Example: Between the hours of 8:00 a.m. (or 0800 hours) and 3:00 p.m. (or 1500 hours) on Friday, 2 July 1960.

Between the hours of 8:00 a.m. on Friday, 2 July 1960 and 3:00 p.m. on Saturday, 3 July 1960.

If the hour limits cannot be fixed, set the inclusive limits by days and dates.

Example: Between Tuesday, 14 June 1960 and Friday, 2 July 1960.

Although it may seem to be overdoing it to write the name of the day, such information may be necessary at a later period and the reader will not have to check back on a calendar.

Indefinite and loose expressions of time should not be used. Never use such expressions as "last week," "yesterday," "two days ago." *Be specific.* Always refer to the exact time, day, and date. Exactness in reporting time will maintain the chronological sequence and is essential when testimony is required. Even though it may seem unnecessary to be specific, don't weaken.

There are several ways in which the WHEN can be reported. If there are department rules, they must be observed. The following is suggested:

Date: 2 July 1960

The advantage of separating the date of the month from the year with the name of the month should be obvious. The chances for confusion are reduced. Avoid setting out dates in numerical fashion, i.e., 7/2/60. A person accustomed to reading date, month, year would get the wrong date. A person may become confused in deciding which is the seventh month. To eliminate the possibility of misinterpretation, the form as illustrated, 2 July 1960, is recommended.

Time: 8:00 a.m. or 0800 hours (if the twenty-four hour clock is used)

Since the military and others used the twenty-four hour time system, the investigator should be informed about it. The time starts at 0001 hours which is one minute after midnight and ends at 2400 hours which is midnight. This system avoids the use of a.m. and p.m. When using the conventional time system, the use of a.m. and p.m. is mandatory. (See pp. 64-65.)

The WHEN should include reference to weather conditions for the specific periods reported. Such reference completes the information about a specific period of time. Weather information may prove to be invaluable in checking events and conditions to determine if there are any discrepancies between statements of witnesses, victims, and others, and physical possibility of the event.

WHERE DID IT HAPPEN?

Where did the offense occur?
Where was the object of the offense?
Where is the object of the offense now?
Where was the object of the offense found?
Where was the perpetrator of the offense?
Where is the suspect now?
Where was the suspect when apprehended?
Over what area did the offense extend?
Where were the witnesses in relation to the crime scene?
Where are the witnesses now?

Where did it happen? includes the specific location of all persons and things which may be in any way related to the offense or occurrence. The investigation report must describe these spatial locations so that there can be no question of their identity. One means of accomplishing accuracy is to be *specific.* Being specific implies the correct use of terms.

Place of Occurrence. In general, the WHERE is the precise type of physical area in which the offense was committed. To arrive at a precise location, address and type of premise are used. A complete mailing address is usually appropriate. As a general rule, addresses should include nearest cross streets.

Example: 631 First St., between Maple and Orchard.

The type of premises indicates necessary supplemental information for the address. For example, if the premises are an apartment building, the number of the apartment is part of the address; if an office building, the number of the office is a part of the address. If there are no numbers for offices or apartments, locate the specific scene by words and sketch.

Premises may include everything from vacant lots to skyscrapers. Most premises can be classified by a general name: auto campgrounds; building under construction; building under destruction; garage; warehouse; apartments; barracks; bungalow court; farmhouse; hotel; single-family residence; two-family residence; office building (describe particular office as to its use: accountant's, attorney's, engineer's, insurance, medical, dental, architect's, etc.); auditorium; dance hall; golf course; alley; street; sidewalk; stores (use to which put); vehicles (from automobile to truck); boats and vessels (from barges to yachts).

Once the general classification of the premises is determined, then complete the specific description and include particularly the use to which the premises are put.

The description of the WHERE of the occurrence of the offense should be so written that a stranger reading the report could find the exact spot in the community.

Place of Apprehension. In addition to locating specifically the premises on which the offense was committed, the WHERE includes the location of place of apprehension of a suspect, the place of location of the property recovered, the location of witnesses and participants, the location of the victim, the location of hideouts, the location of hangouts, etc.

Let us assume a suspect is taken into custody. The exact geographical location of the arrest must be given. If the arrest occurs within a building, the building must be identified generally and specifically with full address. Then the exact place in the building where the arrest was made must be described. If the place is a room, it must be identified by floor, number, and other specific data. The names of onlookers or witnesses should be included.

If the arrest is made on a sidewalk outside a building, the building address is included for location. If made in an alley, parking strip, etc. adjacent to a building, the building address is included.

If an arrest is made at an intersection, name the streets intersecting and describe the geographical spot: northwest corner of 12th and Maple, with any other identifying data.

If the suspect is in jail, *be specific* in stating what jail, name and locate the jail.

If an arrest is made where there is no nearby street number, use descriptive words: west side of Fifth Street, 100 yards north of Orchard Blvd. Or, if a field, 100 yards north of Orchard Blvd. on west side of Fifth Street, 25 feet west of street line.

Location of Recovered Property. In describing the location of recovered property, *be specific.* Identify property and place where recovered. Do not take anything for granted. Do not assume any knowledge on the part of anyone else. Assume you are the only one who has the information. Tell precisely what it was that was recovered and where it was recovered. The purpose of this description is to enable any reader of the report to locate the scene of the recovery and to identify the property.

Location of Witnesses. Witnesses are of no use if they cannot be found. It is therefore essential that the investigator in describing any witness and his testimony must include the full name, sex, occupation, business and home addresses, and any other addresses at which the witnesses may be found. Telephone numbers should be considered as part of any address. Whatever information the investigator thinks will assist in the finding of the witness when needed should be included. Sometimes the above information will not seem to be sufficient; in that case, more will be sought, such as names of friends, acquaintances; name and location of bank with which witness does business; organizations of which witness is a member or officer; description of vehicles which witness owns or which he may use; etc.

Location of Victim. In describing the whereabouts of the victim at the time of the offense, do not rely on the verbal description given by the victim. Have the victim "walk through" what happened. Take him to the scene and have him reenact what occurred there. In this way any discrepancy between statement and physical possibility can be noted. This procedure enables the investigator to check whether or not it was physically possible for something to have occurred about which the victim says he is certain. For example, the victim may say that the perpetrator ran down the street about fifty feet and entered a building. Reenactment may establish that at fifty feet there was no means of entry into a building; neither was there one twenty-five in either direction. It may be that the victim is mistaken, is imagining, or is lying. If such errors are first brought to light on the witness stand during the trial, the investigator, his department, and the prosecution can be made to appear ridiculous.

If the victim does not know precisely where the crime occurred, the answers to some of the following questions are appropriate:

> At what point did the victim become aware of the subject's intent to commit the crime?
>
> At what point was the loss discovered?
>
> At what point was the victim rendered unconscious? Can the victim fix this point with reasonable certainty?
>
> At what point did the victim recover consciousness or was picked up?
>
> At what point did the victim recall suspicious circumstances?
>
> What was the last location the victim can recall with any certainty?

The investigation report will include not only the name of the victim, but a list of all places where he can be found when it may be necessary to get in touch with him.

If the victim is dead, the problem of locating his movements prior to the offense is limited to getting information from relatives, friends, acquaintances, onlookers, witnesses, colleagues, coworkers, etc.

Use of Diagrams, Sketches, Plans, and Photographs. Verbal description can be graphically supplemented by the proper use of diagrams, sketches, plans, and photographs. The use of these aids can assist the investigator during the investigation and can afford others an opportunity to visualize more accurately verbal descriptions.[1]

The officer must be alert to the fact that his only opportunity

[1]Dienstein, William: TECHNICS FOR THE CRIME INVESTIGATOR, Thomas, Springfield, 1952, pp. 26-30.

to find out where he may subsequently locate certain individuals—victims, witnesses, suspects—may be at the time of his arrival at the scene of the offense. The officer at the time of his arrival on the crime scene will ascertain the identity of all persons present, and in describing the WHERE will include with the residence addresses and telephone numbers the names and addresses and telephone numbers of their employers, places of business, or any other places where they may be located at a later date.

HOW DID IT HAPPEN?

How was the offense committed?
> What preparation was made to commit the offense?
> What was done to avoid detection?

How was the property or person attacked?
> What method was used to induce the victim to give up his property?
> What means were used to overcome resistance of the victim?
> What means or instruments were used in the perpetration of the offense?

How did the offender act?
> What method of approach was used in the perpetration of the offense?

How did the victim act?
> What did the victim do in response to the actions of the perpetrator?

How did the situation assist in the commission of the offense?
How did the offender enter the crime scene?
> What means were used?

How did the offender leave the crime scene?
> What means were used?

How did it happen? answers a multitude of detailed questions about the occurrence. It constitutes a major portion of the information included in the report. Having covered the WHO, the persons involved in the occurrence; the WHAT, the offense; the WHEN, the time of the occurrence; and the WHERE, the location of the occurrence; it is necessary to go into the details of HOW the offense was committed. What means were used? What conversation took place? What was the method of procedure or operation of the offender?

In one respect, the HOW is the *modus operandi* of the perpetrator. From the information gained during the process of investigating, how was the offense accomplished? Because the investigator is filled with information about the case, there is the tendency to overlook reporting *all* the details related to the investigation. Whatever crime is being investigated and reported, all the events preceding the offense should be included in the HOW. The kinds of information required in the answering of the HOW will be indicated in the following examples. Since they are only examples, they should not be treated as inclusive for any of the offenses listed. The outlines are merely indicative of what might be included.

Offenses Against Persons. Robbery, assault, battery, murder, kidnaping, abduction, mayhem, sex offenses, extortion.

How did the perpetrator approach the victim?
　　What device, trick, ruse, method did the perpetrator use to gain access to the victim?
How did the perpetrator say?
　　What exact expressions were used?
What in detail did the perpetrator do?
　　How did he act?
What means did he use?

gun	seduction	razor
knife	promise	chemical
bodily force	blackmail	missile
club	poison	badge
intoxication	scissors	request
		other

What preceded the offense?

quarrel	breaking and entering
attack	robbery
accusation	burglary
self-defense	

　　impersonation (officer, repairman, inspector, salesman, prospective renter or buyer, canvasser, etc.)
What was the victim doing immediately preceding and at the time of the offense?
　　opening or closing premises

going to the bank
walking
riding in vehicle
at residence
preparing to leave residence
arriving at residence
parking automobile
other

Were there accomplices?
complete personal descriptions
What did the accomplices do?
How did they participate in the crime?
What was said?
How many were there?
Did they arrive with the perpetrator?
Did they leave with the perpetrator?

How did the perpetrator arrive and depart?

taxi   on foot
automobile   other

What other facts surrounding the occurrence could be used to identify the perpetrator and accomplices?

Offenses Against Property. Burglary, theft, larceny, worthless checks, embezzlement, arson.

Burglary

Precisely what type of premises were entered?
Where was the point of entry?
Where was the point of departure?
What instruments were used to gain entry?
What was done by the investigator to preserve evidence of entry and exit?
What acts were committed by the perpetrator at the scene?
eating
drinking
defecating, urinating
malicious damage
defacing
smoking
use of matches

disturbance of materials
other
Where were occupants of the premises?
  exact location
How did perpetrator arrive and depart?
Any facts or acts that can be used to identify the perpetrator?

Theft, Larceny
  From what place was property stolen?

automobile	room, specific type
basement	showcase
closet	slot machine
counter	store
display stand	telephone box
kitchen	toilet
locker	tool box
lobby	trunk
mail box	vehicle
meter	window
porch: front,	yard
back	other

  Were there occupants on the premises?
    Where were they?
  What means were used to take the property?
    carrying away
    shoplifting
    trick and device
    bodily force
    other
  How did the victim discover the loss?
  What means were used to distract attention of victims or persons in the vicinity?
  How did perpetrator arrive and depart?

Worthless Checks
  How were checks written or otherwise prepared?
    pen
    pencil
    typewriter

check writer
raised
rubber stamp
amount
What type of paper was used?
  printed check form
  printed pay check
  counter check
  money order
  personal check form
How were checks returned?
  not sufficient funds (NFS)
  improper endorsement
  no such account
  forged
  fictitious
What purpose was to be served by check?
  cash, money
  jewelry
  clothing
  merchandise: type
  vehicle
  other
What claim was made by passer to establish authenticity
  of check?
  making purchase as customer
  impersonating another
  exhibits check book, bank deposit book, driver's license,
    other
  refers to well known person or persons
  pretends to live in neighborhood
  uses bogus letter of credit
  other
Was victim able to note description of check passer?
  What caused particular notice?
What did passer say when presenting check to victim?
What time of day was check passed?
How did the check passer arrive and depart?
Other pertinent facts?

Embezzlement

What was the subject of the embezzlement?

What was the value of the property?

Who had ownership?

Who had possession at the time of the conversion?

Under what circumstances was the property received or held?

How was the loss discovered?

Where was the property recovered?

Who had possession at the time of recovery?

(Questions under *Worthless Checks, Theft* or *Larceny* may be applicable to *Embezzlement*)

Arson

How was the fire reported?

means used: telephone, fire alarm box, other

Who reported the fire?

name, address, telephone number, occupation, description of person, circumstances causing person to note fire,

What was noticed in addition to the fire?

When was the fire discovered?

exact time or inclusive period if exact time not determinable

Specify a.m. or p.m.

Who discovered the fire?

name, address, telephone number, occupation, description, etc.

Under what circumstances was the fire discovered?

Where was the person who discovered the fire?

How did he happen to be there?

What type of structure or property was set on fire?

number of stories

approximate dimensions

approximate number of rooms

construction of building: brick, frame, iron, stucco, fireproof, other

factory, warehouse, mill, dwelling, garage, other

Was the building vacant?

length of time

source of information

name and present address of last occupant

Was the building inhabited?

Was a human being in the structure at the time of the fire?

Would an ordinary person have reason to know or suspect the building was inhabited?

Who occupies the building?

What type of business is carried on in the building?

names, addresses, telephone numbers, descriptions of owners of building.

How long has this business been at this location?

names, addresses, telephone numbers, business or occupation, descriptions of all occupants of the building.

Who owns the building?

name, address, age, description, when acquired building

How was the fire started?

What materials, accelerants, and devices were used?

What was the value of the property destroyed?

What were the findings of the arson investigator, of the fire department, and other agencies?

(Such reports are attached as exhibits.)

Was there a burning or charring as distinguished from mere scorching?

What evidence (traces on clothing of suspect or clue materials at the scene) associated the suspect with the scene?

What actions of the suspect offered evidence of criminal intent?

removal of valuable articles

substitutions

ill-feeling, animosity, hostility, hatred toward owner or occupants

unfriendly relations between suspect and occupants

absence of any effort to extinguish fire or turn in alarm

As seen from the above lists, any idiosyncrasy of the perpetrator or any peculiar method of operation, anything which may constitute the "trademark" or peculiarity of the offender and his offense should be included in the HOW of the report. Often one is astonished at the peculiar behavior pattern of an offender in his preparation for an offense, in the commission of the offense, and in his attempts at avoiding detection. Check passers sometimes will use the same amount for each check passed or won't go over a certain amount. The amount of the check becomes the passer's trademark. In other cases, the passer will use exactly the same words during the cashing of a check. Whatever the offender does that marks the offense—the criminal act—with a peculiarity becomes a trademark of the offender. It is a part of the *modus operandi* and is the distinguishing feature that makes this particular offender different from any other offender who commits the same type of offense.

Most police department offense reports and arrest reports (accident, assault, burglary, dead body, forgery, robbery, theft, etc.) are really checklist reports composed of brief fill-in and checklist items. However, these reports do contain a space headed with the title "Remarks" or "Further Details" or something similar. The purpose of such a section of a report form is to provide the officer with an opportunity to indicate any facts pertaining to an arrest or offense which are not covered by the items of the report form or which need more detailed explanation.

The "Remarks" item of the report is the place for narrating additional information which may be of value in providing clues or leads, in more clearly determining the method of operation, in describing events leading up to the offense, and for a complete itemization, description, and valuation of property if not included elsewhere in the report.

The "Remarks" or "Further Details" section of the report provide an opportunity to elaborate and add to the HOW items of the report form. If the officer will consider the printed items of the report as the skeleton and his comments under the "Remarks" section as flesh and blood, he may gain an idea of the value of this particular section and of its purpose. A well-prepared "Remarks" or "Detail" section can provide superior officers in the department with leads as to which officers show aptitude for investigation.

For some reason there is a tendency on the part of many investigators to neglect the HOW section of the report. It seems as if the investigator feels that after showing the WHO, WHAT, WHEN, and WHERE, it makes little difference about the HOW. In neglecting the HOW, the investigator overlooks the fact that he had to find out the HOW before he could fully answer the WHO, WHAT, WHEN, and WHERE. The investigator in knowing the HOW, understands the other four questions. The reader of the report does not know the HOW unless he reads it in the report. It is therefore the responsibility of the investigator to complete his information by describing the HOW in detail.

As noted above, the HOW of a report supplies the information used in maintaining the modus operandi file. For example, an extortioner may accuse his victim of a degenerate act, or may accuse his victim of an unlawful act, or may threaten to reveal some real or alleged act of the victim which would destroy victim's position, prestige, influence, or reputation. Each extortioner develops a pattern of behavior or method that he uses. He seldom deviates. It is possible then to identify an extortioner by his *modus operandi*, the HOW of his offense, providing he has a previous record. If he has no previous record, his next offense will be identifiable. The type of person he picks as a victim, the method he uses, the amount he asks for, all add up to *modus operandi*. *Modus operandi* information is obtained from information detailed under such general headings as: persons attacked, property attacked, how attacked, means of attack, object of attack, trademark, and vehicle used. Unless the investigator is able to dig out the details, he cannot report sufficient information to supply the needed details of the offense to complete the HOW adequately.

The HOW is the basis for the prosecution's case. A case cannot be proved in court by simply stating that the defendant, Abercrombie Jones, did feloniously take and deprive the owner of lawful use of an automobile on 4 July 1960 between the hours of 11:30 a.m. and 1:45 p.m. at Azusa, Montana. The court will want to know the exact details of the theft. Some of the questions that must be answered in court will indicate the amount of detailed information that is required in any investigation report.

Who owns the car?

What proof of ownership is there?

In what condition was the car?
What is the car's description?
From what place was the car taken? When?
  Was it parked on the street? alley? garage?
    parking lot? other?
  What was exact location of car?
  Who put it there?
  Was it lawfully there?
  How did it happen to be there?
  When was it put there?
  How long was it there?
What precautions had been taken to prevent theft?
  Were the keys removed from the ignition?
  Was there an extra set of keys in the car?
  Were all the doors locked?
  Were all the windows rolled up tightly?
  Was it possible to lock the car?
Who discovered the theft?
  How was the theft discovered?
Who reported the theft?
  Under what circumstances was the theft reported?
  When was it reported stolen?
  By whom was it reported?
  To whom was it reported?
  What action was taken based on the theft report?
  When was action taken based on the theft report?
How was the car stolen?
  What method was used to remove the car?
  What efforts were made to conceal the identity of the
    car?
  Where was the car taken?
  What was done with the car?
How was the car recovered?
  Who recovered the car?
  What were the circumstances of recovery?
  Where was the car recovered?
  How was the car identified?
  In what condition was the car?

How was the defendant identified as the thief?
Was he in possession of the car at the time of arrest?
Did he claim ownership?
Had he disposed of the car?
If so, to whom, when, where, and for how much?
Did the buyer know it was a stolen car?
Had the car been taken across a state line?
Who apprehended the defendant?
Under what circumstances was he arrested?
By whom was he arrested?
Where is the car now?

The foregoing outline of questions about a stolen vehicle cover the WHO, WHAT, WHEN, WHERE, and HOW. They illustrate the type of questions which will have to be answered during a prosecution. On the basis of the investigation report in which the answers will appear, the prosecutor knows what to expect and how to proceed. He knows what sort of a case he has. He can be successful in building an adequate case for prosecution only to the degree that *all* the facts are in the report.

3

WHAT ARE THE PRINCIPLES OF GOOD REPORT WRITING?

In SETTING FORTH the WHO, WHAT, WHEN, WHERE and HOW, there are five principles of writing which must be observed in the preparation of every report: *accuracy, completeness, brevity, impartiality,* and *form.* To observe these principles of good report writing, the investigator must know the difference between facts, hearsay, opinions, and conclusions. He must be aware of his own biases and prejudices. He must observe the rules of grammar and punctuation.

HOW CAN ACCURACY BE ACHIEVED IN WRITING A REPORT?

How are facts distinguished from hearsay?
How are facts distinguished from opinion?
How are facts distinguished from conclusions?
How are words used to express facts?

Accuracy is the first principle of good report writing. It is achieved by relating the information about the investigation which was gained through the physical senses—sight, smell, taste, hearing, and touch. The report is a complete recitation of the relevant knowledge obtained during the investigation without any subtraction or addition. If anything has been added or subtracted, intentionally or not, consciously or unconsciously, the writer has not reported accurately. The personal integrity of the investigator is reflected in the accuracy of his report.

Every investigator will feel that his report is accurate and that he would not sign an inaccurate report. However, it is difficult to attain complete accuracy in a report. There are weaknesses and limitations in all of us that make the task more difficult. First, we must know our weaknesses and limitations; then we must take such measures as tend to reduce their effect on whatever we do. Our weaknesses and limitations usually are outgrowths of strong feelings we tend to have about persons, places, ideas, and things. Strong feelings tend to distort objective description. Feelings may cause us to make snap judgments, judgments more in keeping with our feelings than with the realities. Strong feelings may cause us to seek evidence that will support our feelings and reject evidence that will not support them. Or strong feelings may cause us to misinterpret evidence. Our feelings are reflected in our biases, prejudices, habits, and emotional reactions. Our limitations are reflected in our physical and mental condition. These are the things we must know about ourselves.

Second, we must be aware continually of the following:

1. the distinction between fact and hearsay,

2. the distinction between fact and opinion,

3. the distinction between fact and conclusion, and

4. the meanings of the words we use: the meanings other people give these words; the meanings we give them.

Fact vs. Hearsay. A fact is that which an investigator has learned through the use of his own five senses. A fact is that which the investigator has heard, has seen, has tasted, has smelled, has touched. The fact is the personal knowledge gained by the investigator at firsthand from the situation through his senses. Hearsay is all other information. Hearsay is learned secondhand by the investigator. Statements from other persons, even those of eye-witnesses, are hearsay. Herein lies a basic source of confusion: confusion between the fact of a statement and the reliability and validity of a statement. An example may clarify this issue.

A report states that Abercrombie Jones was born in Azusa, Montana, on 4 July 1940. There is no other information about the birth of Abercrombie. Now the writer could not possibly know that Abercrombie was born in the place and at the time stated unless he were present at the birth or saw the birth certificate. Let us assume that the investigator obtained this information from Abercrombie during the course of an interrogation. Therefore, an accurate report is "Abercrombie Jones stated to this officer during an interview held in Room 1A, City Hall,

Maple City, on 5 July 1960, that he was born in Azusa, Montana, on 4 July 1940.

The fact is that Abercrombie made a statement to the officer about his birthdate and birthplace. The content of the statement is hearsay. It is easy to take the statements of others and convert them into facts through continuous use and thinking about the statement. If, while organizing and preparing the report, the writer will keep in mind the WHO, WHAT, WHEN, WHERE, and HOW *as they relate to him,* he will remain aware of what information he obtained through his five senses and what information was furnished to him by someone else. The information furnished by others is hearsay.

The four W's and the H as they relate to the investigator may be indicated as follows:

> Whom did the investigator see? hear? smell? touch?
> What did the investigator see? hear? smell? taste? touch?
> When did the investigator see? hear? smell? taste? touch?
> Where did the investigator see? hear? smell? taste? touch?
> How did the investigator see? hear? smell? taste? touch?

In an investigation report, accuracy is achieved by reporting fact as fact and hearsay as hearsay. This is accomplished by relating how the information was obtained, whether by the investigator through his five senses or through another person or source. Being continuously aware of the source of the information will enable the investigator to distinguish between fact and hearsay.

In gathering and reporting information from witnesses, suspects, victims, all of which is hearsay information, the officer should again use the four W's and H as a guide. A reporting of hearsay evidence to be complete should include:

> Who is the source of the information?
> > Who is the informant?
> > A complete description that will identify the source is required.
> What information was obtained?
> > What was told to the investigator by the informant? If the information is obtained in the field, the investigator may be unable to accomplish a verbatim report. He will then be restricted to notes about who was involved, what

happened, when it happened, where it happened, how
it happened, *all from the viewpoint of the informant.*
When was the information obtained?
   When did the informant provide the investigator with
   the information? time and date (usually inclusive pe-
   riods of time)
Where was the information obtained?
   Where did the informant tell the investigator the in-
   formation? exact place, location, address
How was the information obtained?
   What were the circumstances attendant to obtaining
   the information?
   What brought about the telling?
   Who was present at the time of the telling?
   Were there interruptions? By whom or by what?
   What was the demeanor of the informant at the time of
   the telling?

In reporting hearsay, the hearsay information is preceded by
the source, or if the source is unidentified, by the phrase, "unidentified source." The contents of the informant's statements are
hearsay. That a statement was made to the investigator or in his
presence is a fact.

Facts vs. Opinions. Since a fact is that which can be observed
through one or more of the five senses, it is something that is
verifiable; that is, someone else can repeat the act and report the
same or similar information. A fact has the quality of being independent of any single person or observation. It is an actuality
open to the scrutiny of others. The essence of a fact lies in its
verifiability; that is, it can be confirmed or substantiated.

An opinion is what a person thinks or believes about something. It is a personal estimation approximating a judgment, but
falls short of the certainty of conviction usually attributed to a
judgment. It is an idea, an impression, or a notion resulting from
a personal sentiment and usually involves a liking or disliking, a
favorable or unfavorable estimation, a positive or negative attitude.

Opinions are formed consciously or unconsciously; we may be
aware or unaware that the process of forming an opinion has oc-

curred. There is nothing inhuman about forming opinions. It is the fact of their existence that concerns us, especially the investigator. For he must be able to distinguish whether what he thinks is an opinion or a fact; whether what he hears is someone's opinion or observation. The distinction can be made by applying the guide of the WHO, WHAT, WHERE, WHEN and HOW. Unless the investigator can distinguish between fact and opinion, he cannot write an accurate report.

Opinions of the investigator are not a part of the report, nor do they have a place in the report, unless it is the policy of the department to permit the expression of opinion in specifically designated paragraphs of the report titled "Opinion." Where reports provide for an expression of opinion, it usually is limited to the investigator's estimation of the credibility of the various informants. Any such estimation should be preceded by the phrase, "It is the opinion of this investigator . . ." An opinion is an opinion because there is insufficient evidence to support it. For this reason, the opinions of the investigator usually are not given in the written report.

The foregoing discussion does not imply that the investigator will not have opinions during the course of an investigation. His opinions may serve as guides for further action when he seems to have reached a dead end. He may conduct various aspects of his investigation on the basis of opinions. But it is important for him to recognize that he is acting on the basis of opinion and he must not forget it. When he does forget, he is engaging in fantasy instead of approaching reality, and his report misleads the reader.[1]

Fact vs. Conclusion. The word conclusion is one of a group

[1]*Chicago American*:Friday, July 21, 1961, page 14, excerpt from an editorial:

". . . His report, though, didn't seem like the result of an impartial investigation; it sounded more like an impassioned plea for the defense. It contained biting remarks about 'back fence' gossip and unfounded rumor; and made all kinds of assumptions to favor the accused men. For instance, ———— stated that both men had good records, and so would have risked their careers by taking bribes. This is conjecture, and doesn't belong in a factual report. Neither does his claim that the bribery charges couldn't be true because, if it (sic) had been, city officials would have acted long ago—a piece of reasoning that seems downright naive."

This excerpt reveals how an investigator can discredit his investigation by failing to differentiate fact, opinion, and conclusion.

of nouns that relates to formulations derived by reason. The other words in the group are inference, deduction, and judgment. A conclusion involves the drawing of an inference that is or appears to be the necessary and logical consequence of preceding propositions, information, or evidence. For example, arriving at the scene of a homicide, the officer finds the body of a woman and a man with a gun in his hand. The preceding statement may be put in the following manner: There is a dead body. The man has a gun in his hand. The man committed a homicide. The last sentence is a conclusion.

Stated as above, the reader will recognize that the conclusion is not a fact. It is quite possible that the man is the husband of the victim who rushed into the room on hearing the sound of gun fire, saw the gun, picked it up, and stood as if in a trance over the body of his wife. Or it may be that the man fired the gun at the wall to show it was not loaded and the woman died of a heart attack. In either set of circumstances, the conclusion is invalid and is not a fact, although the reasoning is logical.

Examination of the tableau presented reveals the following facts:

1. The body of a woman is lying on the floor.

2. A man with a gun in his hand is standing in the room.
The arriving officer, on viewing the tableau, may jump to a number of conclusions based on the above two facts:

1. Seeing the man with a gun in his hand may result in the conclusion that the man recently fired it at the victim.

2. Seeing the body may result in the conclusion that the bullet from the gun struck the victim causing fatal injury.

3. Converting conclusions 1 and 2 into premises, it logically may be concluded that the man is the killer:

    a. The man fired the gun.

    b. The woman lies dead from a gunshot wound.

    c. The man was the killer.

The foregoing example is presented to make the point that it is possible to draw faulty conclusions from facts. On the other hand, it is possible to draw valid conclusions from opinions, guesses, invalid statements, or assumptions. In neither instance is the conclusion a fact until verification is made through further information, data, and evidence.[1]

A fact proves itself. A conclusion requires corroborative evidence. A fact is observable. A conclusion is reasoned. A fact is a reality. A conclusion is a mental construction. A fact exists independently of the observer. A conclusion exists only in the mind of the observer.

The distinction is important. The investigator must be able to separate fact from conclusion and report the fact only. When he confuses fact with conclusion, accuracy in reporting disappears.

Use of Words. In the writing of a report, the officer must keep in mind that he possesses information that the reader does not have. The reader is dependent upon the report for information. Information is communicated through the use of words. Words have meanings. These meanings are not inherent in the word. Meanings are given to words by people. Words are symbols: they stand for or represent something. Just as a map represents a bit of geography, so a word represents something. Just as the map is not the geographical area it represents, so the word is not the something for which it stands.

A word that has a particular meaning for the writer may have another meaning for the reader. A combination of words or a single word may evoke a picture in the mind of the reader that was not intended by the writer. This puts the burden upon the report writer of doing everything within his capacity to make certain the words he uses to convey his information will be interpreted as intended. The problem of making oneself understood through the medium of words is complicated by a number of factors. A complete discussion of these factors is beyond the scope of this presentation.

For the purpose of this monograph a few comments must suffice. First, we must be aware of the fact that some words are emotionally "charged." These may be the "fighting" or insulting

---

[1]The fact that police practice requires that the arriving officer must react to the tableau as presented *as if* the man with the gun were the killer does not invalidate the presentation. The police officer must protect himself and must disarm the man.

words of children and adolescents. Among adults the charged words will vary from time to time. Sometimes we use charged words as adjectives to modify nouns when we feel strongly about the topic. (Examples: friendly, heinous, brutal, callous, perverted.) Sometimes we use nouns that have negative connotations. Words like beatnik, bum, hood, punk, fiend, killer, sexmaniac evoke negative images of the person so described. It may be that the person described is all these things. But a good report will describe the person as male, white, unkempt, unshaven, dressed in soiled sweat shirt and soiled jeans, wearing worn, dirty, white tennis shoes. By using "loaded" or "charged" words in a report, except when quoting statements, the report writer is violating the principle of accuracy because the words used describe the writer's response to the situation rather than a description of the object observed.

Second, we must also be aware that words can evoke images in the reader unrelated to the report. The kind of images evoked depend upon the past experiences of the reader, and these experiences are not necessarily the same as those of the writer. For example, the word "home" denotes a place where one lives with his family. This is a fixed definition. But the word "home" may connote several different ideas or emotions that have been added to it or attached to it because of a variety of experiences. To one person, "home" connotes, intimacy, privacy, pleasant associations; to another, "home" connotes bickering, quarreling, deprivation. To one, it connotes a rambling, vine-covered cottage; to another, a tar-paper shack.

The report writer should avoid the use of words that may produce a connotation which overshadows the denotation. He should use words that tend to maintain dictionary definitions, rather than words which are given meanings not found in the dictionary. Slang terms, vernacular terms, jargon should be avoided. He should avoid words whose meanings tend to vary with different groups of people. The investigator is usually on the safe side when he uses simple, direct language, selecting his words carefully, if necessary with the use of a dictionary. When in doubt as to whether or not a particular word will communicate the meaning intended, have another person read the sentence or paragraph and explain what it means to him.

By using words that tend to have precise definitions and by constructing sentences so that there is but one interpretation, the report writer will be limiting the possibility of making vague, obscure, doubtful, questionable, and ambiguous statements.

HOW CAN COMPLETENESS BE ACHIEVED IN WRITING A REPORT?

How is incompleteness recognized?
How is incomplete information handled?
How are undeveloped leads included?
How do we know the report is complete?

Completeness is the second principle of good report writing. It is achieved by narrating all the facts discovered during the course of the investigation. Herein lies one of the reasons that many investigative reports fall short of their purpose. The investigator reminds himself that, of course, he must report all the facts, but the facts reported must be relevant to the case being investigated. He cannot include everything. Therefore, he will leave out data which he considers irrelevant. What may appear irrelevant in the writing of a preliminary report may turn out to be essential in building the case. What may appear to be irrelevant to the investigator may be relevant to the reviewer or to the prosecutor. In short, in the initial reports particularly, the investigator cannot know what information will be relevant and what will be irrelevant. The general rule is this: When in doubt, include the information.

The writer of a report must not leave anything to the imagination of the reader. He must not assume that the reader will read "between the lines," or will understand without being specifically told. In the first place, the writer cannot assume that the reader knows anything about the case. The report must be written on the premise that the reader knows nothing about the case, never heard of the case, never heard anything about the persons, places, or facts involved, and never heard of the writer of the report. Many investigators will think this assumption unwarranted since they have discussed the case with their superior. be aware of the general activities of the investigator, he himself But the fact remains that although the immediate superior may is not making the investigation. He is supervising or directing it. In addition, the report doesn't stop with the immediate superior. It may go to many others for review. The investigator or his superior cannot go along with the report to explain and orally add to its contents. The report must be as complete as the status of the investigation makes it possible.

There is a general tendency for people to overlook the reality that partially stated facts can be as misleading as falsehoods. A partial narration can create a false picture in the mind of the writer as well as the mind of the reader. Decisions based upon an incomplete statement of facts without pointing out that the statement is incomplete may lead to the making of erroneous decisions which can make the personnel involved appear to be ridiculous and even incompetent. The reader of the report will know only as much about the case as is reported. He will make a decision solely on what he reads in the report. Unless the information reported appears to be incomplete on its face, the reader cannot assume that the writer has withheld information, or failed to secure information, or has inadvertently omitted information.

An incomplete reporting of information basic to an investigation can bring about an injustice not only to the subject, but to the investigator, his colleagues and his superior, his division, and his department.

Incomplete Information. If the investigator knows that certain information is lacking, he should report:

    1. What information is lacking or is incomplete,

    3. What efforts were made to obtain this information,

    3. Why the information was not obtained, and

    4. What must be done to obtain this information.

Undeveloped Leads. If the investigator is aware of possible sources of information which he has not contacted, he should set them out in detail. He should state why the source is sought and what information might be available. The writer should describe all the avenues of inquiry which were considered so as to allow the reviewer to decide whether or not the undeveloped leads should be followed especially if further action requires the assistance of other agencies.

HOW CAN BREVITY BE ACHIEVED IN WRITING
A REPORT?

How is brevity consistent with completeness?
How is brevity consistent with accuracy?
How is brevity related to information about the investigation?
How is brevity related to the use of language?

Brevity is the third principle of good report writing. It is achieved by keeping out of the report unnecessary detail. Although it may appear at first glance that completeness and brevity are inconsistent, there is really no conflict between the two principles. Completeness requires the inclusion of all relevant, pertinent, and essential information. Brevity requires the exclusion of all unrelated, extraneous, incidental, and nonessential information and unnessary detail.

To achieve brevity, knowledge of sentence and paragraph structure is essential. Every sentence must have a subject and a verb and must express a complete idea. (See pp. 48-50.) Every paragraph must be about a single idea. (See p. 50.) The writer must avoid the use of words that are open to more than one interpretation. (See pp. 39-41.) The writer must avoid the use of numerous adjectives; he must avoid useless repetition. Repetition is effective only when used as a means of impressing upon the listener an idea during a lecture or exposition. Avoid slang unless it is part of a quoted statement. Avoid attempts at wit, sarcasm, flowery expressions.

Brevity in a report can be achieved by avoiding the use of too many words. By using too many words the writer not only loses his reader but also loses himself. It is not unusual for information to be hidden with too many words. A general rule is this: When you have a choice between saying the same thing in one sentence or two sentences, say it in one sentence. When you have a choice of saying the same thing in one word or two words, say it in one word.

Brevity in a report is achieved by avoiding the use of unnecessary adjectives. The uncritical use of adjectives will give the reader the notion that the investigator is trying to slant his report one way or another.

Brevity can be accomplished by avoiding repetition when reference to the matter is sufficient. Instead of repeating a matter each time it is mentioned in the report, after its first complete presentation, the matter when mentioned again should refer to the place in the report where it was initially and completely presented.

In order to achieve brevity, there must be unity, coherence, and emphasis in a good report. Unity refers to a singleness of thought and purpose. The report is the narration of an investigation of a particular offense. Everything in it points to an exposition of that offense. The report has unity when it combines all of its parts into an effective whole. If a reader has to ask, "Why is this included?" there is a lack of unity. Every part of the report combines with every other part to elucidate the offense and its participants.

Coherence refers to continuity and understandability. A report is coherent when it is clear and manifest. There should be no question in the mind of the reader what the report is about, what the investigator did, and what he discovered. There should be a continuity of the parts of the report in that a process is revealed in all its relationships. There should be understandability in that the reader should get a clear notion or idea or image of the investigation. Unity and coherence are not achieved when the report is rambling, wordy, and filled with unnecessary detail. Brevity is essential. Brevity aids in developing unity and coherence, and without unity and coherence, brevity is useless.

Emphasis is an essential characteristic of a good report because it gives weight and/or easy visibility to that which the investigator deems more important. Emphasis may be accomplished by various devices. Form, arrangement, headings, paragraphing, sentence structure, indentation, underlining, and capitalization are some of the ways in which contents in a report may be emphasized and are discussed in a following section. (See pp. 60-66.) Proper uses of devices which provide for emphasis in a report will be consistent with the principle of brevity and will make it easier to be brief. For example, the capitalizing of all the letters in a name makes it easier for the reader to refer to the names in a case.

The report writer should not worry about the length of his report. A lengthy report does not prove that the investigator did a good job. Nor does a short report prove that he did a poor job. The officer should say what he has to say as briefly and as completely as possible and stop. He should not ramble on with inconsequential detail which is of no relevance to the facts being presented and to the case as a whole.

The writer should test his report for completeness and for brevity by asking:

1. Are all the essentials included? (Are the questions WHO, WHAT, WHEN, WHERE, HOW answered?)

2. Are all non-essentials omitted? (Is everything included fundamental to the answering of the WHO, WHAT, WHEN, WHERE, HOW?)

HOW CAN IMPARTIALITY BE ACHIEVED IN WRITING A REPORT?

Impartiality is the fourth principle of good report writing. It is achieved by reporting *all* the facts without any addition or subtraction. It is achieved by the investigator who is aware that his role as an investigator is that of a fact finder and narrator of all information he has acquired.

Impartiality is achieved when nothing is concealed or withheld because it may tend to weaken a case or because it doesn't happen to fit the preconceived notion held by the investigator. Withholding a fact or bit of information in a report is a cardinal sin in any investigation. What happens in any case depends upon what is included in the investigative report. If prosecution is instituted, the prosecutor must know *both* the strength and weakness of the case. If the investigator must testify in a weak case, the prosecutor must be fully informed on the weak points.

Impartiality can be achieved by the investigator maintaining an unbiased and open mind about the case. He should take the facts as he finds them. If he must have theories, let the theories be based on the facts and not the facts on the theories. Preconceived ideas about the guilt of the offender, theories based on guesses, on prejudice, on bias often cause the investigator either consciously or unconsciously to warp, twist, and even to concoct facts to fit his previous ideas. Worse yet, it causes him to overlook facts that tend to disprove his position. If the investigator will remember that his job is to find all the facts, he can reduce the chances of falling into this trap.

All of us have biases of one sort or another. We have strong feelings, either positive or negative, about certain persons, groups, events, and ideas. Because we have this strong *for* or *against* feeling, we tend to have for or against predispositions to respond toward certain persons, groups, events, objects and ideas. Unless we are aware of these emotional predispositions we will react to the feeling we already possess rather than to the reality with which we are confronted. We must therefore examine ourselves and become aware of our biases so that we can counterbalance them and thereby reduce the hazard of being led on a false trail because of our strong feelings. (Here a caution must be interjected. The investigator may be convinced that his strong feeling about something or someone is justified by his experience. But the investigator must not fall into the easy way of assuming that his experiences and his interpretation of them are sufficient evidence to warrant a prejudgment about another situation).

If the investigator will keep in mind continually that his job is to find out what happened, how it happened, where it happened, when it happened, and who is involved, he can reduce the influence of his biases and prejudices.

The investigator is one who investigates, one who scrutinizes, studies, probes, searches; one who examines and inquires with systematic attention and observation to detail and relationship. The aim of an investigation is to uncover facts that lead to the establishment of a case. The investigator is neither prosecutor nor judge. He is neither antagonist nor protagonist. Should the investigator assume any role other than that of fact-finder, his functioning in his role as investigator is impaired. He must not make prejudgments and decide in advance who is guilty and who is innocent, who shall or shall not be prosecuted, and what the penalty should be. These are not his functions. The investigator who tries to prove his prejudices is a liability to himself, to his colleagues, and to his department.

One other factor that tends to influence the impartiality of a report is the situation in which an investigator becomes emotionally involved in the process of seeking information. When this occurs, the effectiveness of the inquiry becomes clouded because emotional attachment or rejection reduces the investigator's capability to view objectively, to observe, and to analyze. If the officer will keep in mind that a criminal offense is an injury to society and not an affront to him, he can reduce the possibility of personalizing crimes.

HOW CAN PROPER FORM BE ACHIEVED IN WRITING A REPORT?

How can a report be made easy to read?
How can it be determined what abbreviations to use?
How are numbers used in a report?
How are the rules of capitalization, paragraphing, punctuation, composition, and grammar applied?

Form is the fifth essential of good report writing. It is achieved by arranging the contents of the report in such a way as to enable the reader to identify quickly any section, part, or item. Form refers to the disposition of the material presented, the visual arrangement of the material, and the mechanical layout. Anything that will make the report easier to read may be considered under form. Observing the rules of grammar and composition improves form. For example, proper paragraphing, correct sentence structure, proper indentation, proper underlining, proper capitalization, and proper abbreviation will improve form. Any device which arranges the various parts or items of the report relates to the form of the report.

Form includes the presentation of the various sections of the report identified with headings, with the relevant material under each heading, and with pages numbered. Form refers to spelling, punctuation, clarity and preciseness of expression, and the proper inclusion of exhibits. If the report can be read easily and understood without several rereadings, if the reader can find the parts in which he is primarily interested without difficulty, then the report form is adequate.

The form of a report may be likened to directional signs on

a road. Directional signs guide the person to his destination. They facilitate his movement. The form of a report serves a similar purpose; it informs the reader where he is, what each section is about, and what comes next; it facilitates the reader's movement through the report. Just as directional signs are standardized, so should the report form be standardized in order that each device used can be recognized without the need for interpretation.

Language Guide for Report Writing. Since we use words to convey our thoughts and ideas, it is obvious why we have "dictionary definitions" of words. For the same reason we have rules about how to use these words and how to put them together to form complete thoughts. Without these definitions and rules, it would be impossible for people to communicate effectively. What follows should not be construed as being an inclusive text on functional grammar and usage. A few aspects have been selected for attention. The reader is urged to become familiar with the various English texts and handbooks and select as a reference one which appeals to him. (A few are listed in the Reference List.)

Sentence Structure

In the English language all complete thoughts are usually expressed through what is called a sentence. A sentence is an arrangement of words having two parts, a part that names something which is called the subject and a part that asserts something about the thing named which is called the verb. Every sentence must contain a subject and a verb. The subject of the sentence is that about which something is said. The verb of a sentence tells what the subject is doing or being.

Example: The victim screamed. "Victim" is the subject; "screamed" is the verb.

Whether the grouping of words numbers three as used in the illustration or as many as fifty, that grouping is not a sentence unless it contains both a subject and a verb. A subject may be composed of one or more words; a verb may be composed of one or more words. Unless a sentence is properly constructed, it does not represent a complete thought. If it is not a complete thought, it cannot be communicated specifically. Writing a clear, concise sentence that communicates a specific thought or observation is the goal of the report writer. A general rule is to keep the sentences short. In this way, the possibility of confusion is reduced.

In a report, the writer should not make it necessary for the reader to insert or add any words whatever in order to complete the sentence or to make it communicable. It is difficult enough for a reader to grasp the meaning intended by the writer without requiring the reader to insert or add words in order to give the writer's statement meaning. It is too easy to add the wrong word. How often do we hear the lament, "I thought he meant thus an so instead of so and thus!"

A sentence, like the report, must have unity, coherence, and emphasis. A sentence that has unity expresses a complete thought. If it expresses a fragmentary or partial thought or idea, the words do not constitute a sentence. One of the most frequent errors in sentence structure is the use of a sentence fragment as a complete sentence.

> *Sentence Error:* He continued along the highway. Although he intended to turn off.

If the reader will read aloud the first grouping of words followed by a period, he will find that the words make sense and express a complete idea. If he will read aloud the second grouping of words followed by a period, he will find that the words do not make complete sense. Something more is needed. The second grouping of words illustrates the sentence fragment. It belongs to the first grouping of words as a modifying and subordinate part.

> *Correct Sentence:* He continued along the highway although he intended to turn off.

Another variation of this partial construction is illustrated by the use of a dependent clause as a sentence:

> While waiting for the subject to appear.

The idea written is fragmentary. Something must follow to complete the thought.

> While waiting for the SUBJECT to appear, the officer observed a disturbance on the premises.

The second major form of sentence error is running two or more sentences together. Usually the error is the result of failing to punctuate between sentences.

> The witnesses reported to the precinct captain they were requested to observe several persons seated in the interview room none of the persons observed were known to the witnesses.

In the foregoing illustration, three separate and distinct ideas are run together. Correctly written they would be punctuated as follows:

> The witnesses reported to the precinct captain. They were requested to observe several persons seated in the interview room. None of the persons observed were known to the witnesses.

A sentence that has coherence is arranged in such a manner that each word is so related to adjacent words as to make the meaning perfectly clear.

A sentence that has proper emphasis is so arranged that the subject and verb are obvious.

Paragraphs

The paragraph exemplifies the basic subdivision of any writing. A paragraph is made up of one or more sentences which develop a single idea or topic. The paragraph is often introduced with a sentence which presents the topic to be discussed. The other sentences in the paragraph develop the topic. The paragraph usually is identified by the indentation of the first sentence. This indentation enables the reader to pick out an item of information more easily. It also imposes upon the writer the responsibility of grouping his sentences in a careful and proper manner so that each paragraph discusses only a single topic that the reader can readily identify.

Numbering paragraphs permits easy reference to specific topics throughout the report by merely citing a number.

The paragraph, like the sentence, must have unity, coherence and emphasis. A paragraph has unity when every sentence bears directly upon the topic presented by the initial sentence in that particular paragraph. Any departure from the specific topic requires a new paragraph.

A paragraph has coherence when the arrangement of the

sentences in the paragraph is such that each thought expressed leads to the next thought.

A paragraph has emphasis when it is introduced with a sentence which presents the topic to be discussed.

Short paragraphs make for easier reading of the report as well as for easier comprehension.

Abbreviations

An abbreviation represents a contraction of a word by omitting some of its letters or by substituting a symbol. The abbreviation saves space and avoids repetition of long words or titles and the like. However, there is always the danger that the reader will misunderstand the abbreviation or will lose time and continuity in reading while trying to ascertain its meaning.

Writers fall into the habit of abbreviating certain words and titles and assume that the abbreviation is self-evident to the reader. What may seem self-evident to the writer may not be self-evident to the reader. The safest procedure is to abbreviate only those words and titles for which standardized abbreviations have been prepared by the department. The source of approved abbreviations is the dictionary. If a report is to go outside the department, it is well to avoid all abbreviations. The amount of space or time saved by using abbreviations may be offset by misunderstanding and misinterpretation.

Capitalization

The following is a basic list of rules governing capitalization which may be useful in narrative report writing:

Capitalize the first word of every sentence.

Capitalize the first word of the direct quotation or direct question.

Example: The hold-up man said, "Line up against the wall."

Capitalize the names of particular persons, places, or things.

real or fictitious names of persons

names of days of the week, names of special holidays, names of the months

names of schools and colleges

names of streets

titles of organizations, associations, groups

names of countries, states, cities, countries

names of oceans, rivers, lakes, mountains, dams, forests

words derived from proper names

Example: California, Californian

Capitalize some abbreviations.

Example: N.W., S.E., C.O.D., No., (See dictionary.)

Capitalize titles used with proper names.

Example: Jones preferred to be called Sergeant Jones.

Capitalize trade names.

Capitalize titles of publications, documents, movies, plays, programs, magazines, pamphlets, and underline them.

Capitalize the initials of a name.

Capitalize east, west, north, and south only when used to refer to a section of the country.

Example: He came from the South.

He drove off heading south.

The names of the seasons are not capitalized ordinarily.

Example: Some like winter better than fall.

Capitalize names of nationalities and religions.

Numbers

The purpose of having a uniform way of presenting numbers is to reduce the possibility of error in writing or reading.

The date of the month and the year should be written in figures.

Example: 9 Sept. 1961

If a sentence begins with a number it is spelled out. Premise numbers or addresses are written in figures. Spell out numbers one through nine.

Use figures for numbers having two or more digits.

The dollar ($) sign is not used for sums less than $1.00.

Example: He took 65 cents.

Sixty-five cents was taken. (See rule above.)

Pronouns

A pronoun is a word used to take the place of or stand for a noun. It is used ordinarily to avoid repeating names and words.

However, the indiscriminate use of pronouns can lead to much confusion. It must be remembered that pronouns cannot stand alone; they must refer to precedent nouns for identification.

Example: The SUBJECT told JONES that he would meet him at 9:00 p.m. at First and Oak Streets.

The pronouns "he" and "him" can refer to SUBJECT or JONES. To reduce the possibility of this type of confusion, it is suggested that whenever possible repeat the noun instead of using the pronoun even though it may appear to be awkward.

Example: The SUBJECT said to JONES that SUBJECT would meet JONES at 9:00 p.m. at First and Oak Streets.

Punctuation

Punctuation is a part of the mechanics of language and is a device used to clarify the meaning of writing. The purpose of punctuation is to make it easier to comprehend the written words.

The general principles governing the use of punctuation marks are:

If the use of the punctuation mark does not clarify the text, it should be omitted.

In choosing the kind of punctuation mark to use and where to place the mark, the writer's sole aim is to bring out his thoughts more clearly. His decision, however, should be consistent with the rules.

End Marks

Every sentence is ended with a mark.

A period (.) is used to end a declarative sentence, one that makes an ordinary statement.

A question mark (?) is used to end a sentence that asks a question.

An exclamation point (!) is used to end a sentence that expresses strong feeling.

Parentheses ( )

Parentheses are used to enclose matter illustrative of the thought or to enclose matter not an essential part of the main thought as an aside, an explanation, or addition.

Words enclosed in parentheses within a sentence do not

begin with a capital and do not end with any punctuation mark unless the enclosure constitutes a question; then a question mark is used.

If the parenthetical element concludes the sentence, the period is placed outside the parenthesis.

Example: The victim reached for a weapon (a .38 caliber revolver).

Apostrophe '

The apostrophe is used to indicate the omission of letters from words. When used to indicate the omission of a letter from a word, the apostrophe is placed above the point of omission.

Example: When the apartment was revisited on Saturday, 10 September 1960, at 10:00 a.m., JONES wasn't there.

The apostrophe is used with *s* to denote the plurals of letters, figures, signs, symbols, and words used merely as words.

Examples: The *a's* were battered; the *4's* were out of line; the *$'s* were uneven; the *&'s* were slanted; the *and's* were difficult to read.

The apostrophe is used to form the possessive of nouns.

Examples: The SUBJECT'S car was blue and gray. The children's bicycles were damaged.

If the word ends with an *s*, the possessive is formed by adding only the apostrophe.

Examples: JONES' car was stolen on Saturday, 10 September 1960, in the morning between 9:00-11:30 a.m. while parked in front of 224 West North Street.
The boys' scooters were alike.

Do not use the apostrophe with such possessive pronouns as his, ours, yours, theirs, its (as distinguished from the contraction it is—it's). The possessive pronoun stands for the person who possesses the thing and for the thing possessed.

Example: This gun is his.

Colon :

The colon is used to formally introduce a list, a statement, a question, a series of statements or questions, or a long quotation.

The expressions as follows, the following, and the like usually precede the colon in a listing.

> *Example:* The following contraband was found: guns, knives, and clubs.

The colon is also used after the salutation in a business letter (Dear Sir:) and between numerals denoting time (9:30 a.m.).

Comma ,

The comma is a mark used to indicate the separation of words, phrases, or clauses. It makes a slight separation or pause. Listed are some suggestions for its use:

Use a comma to separate the items of a series of words, phrases, or clauses.

> *Example:* Weapons found in the automobile included tire irons, chains, clubs, blackjacks, and revolvers.

Use a comma to set off *yes, no, well,* when used at the beginning of a sentence.

Use a comma between short independent clauses of a compound sentence if they are joined by *but, for, or, yet, and.*

Use a comma to set off items in a date.

> *Examples:* Wednesday, 13 July 1960
> Wednesday, July 13, 1960

Use commas to set off expressions within a sentence which tend to be parenthetical such as persons addressed, appositions, items in addresses and dates, independent phrases and clauses.

> *Examples:* Will you help me, Officer, to find my car?
> JANE SMITH, the victim's wife, stated she had been visiting her mother.
> JOHN SMITH was born on 12 June 1928 in Los Angeles, California.
> JOHN SMITH was born June 12, 1928 in Los Angeles, California.

Use a comma when the introductory clause of a sentence begins with *after, although, as, because, before, if, since, so that, than, though, unless, until, when, whenever, where, wherever, while, why.*

> *Example:* When Officer JONES arrived, the premises were ablaze.

When the adverbial clause follows the main clause, the comma is usually omitted.

Example: The premises were ablaze when Officer JONES arrived.

Use a comma to set off nonessential phrases or clauses within a sentence, that is, a phrase or clause which, if omitted, would not change the meaning of the sentence.

Example: ROBERT N. JONES, Badge number 613, the arrest-officer, was injured.

Use a comma between an office or officer and the name of an organization.

Example: JOHN JONES was president, American Society of Criminology.

Use a comma before *Sr.* and *Jr.* in a name and before a title following a name.

Example: JOHN JONES, SR., President, American Society of Criminology, was from the West.

Use a comma only when it adds to clarity of expression. If used, it should be consistent with the general rules presented.

Dash —

The dash is a line used in punctuation to interrupt a sentence or to set off parts of a sentence. A dash is longer than a hyphen; in typewriting, two hyphens in sequence are used as a dash mark.

A dash is not a substitute for end punctuation.

A dash may be used instead of parentheses to indicate interjections into the sentence.

Example: Whatever the offender does that marks the offense—the criminal act—with a peculiarity becomes a trademark of the offender.

A dash is used to denote hesitancy, a sudden change in ideas, a breaking off.

Examples: The SUBJECT said, "I — I — I'm not going to talk any more."
"It was — no, let's not go into that."
"Sure, I was there, but —."

A dash is used to denote the omission of words, letters, or figures. In quoting directly from a source where parts are missing, the dash may be used.

Example: On the victim's body the following note was found:
"Meet me at 225 North Elm Ave., at — (Remainder of
the note was torn from the paper.)

A dash may be used for emphasis of appositives.

Example: For the amount in the cash register—two dollars—he
killed.

Italics

One line is drawn under words, phrases, or sentences to indicate that they are to be printed in *italics*.

Use italics to indicate the titles of newspapers, books, magazines, paintings, and ships.

Use italics to point out or distinguish words or phrases for
the purpose of emphasis.

Example: He kept pronouncing *persuade* as if it were spelled
persuage.

Use italics to indicate foreign words or phrases which have
not become a part of the English language. (For determination,
use the dictionary.)

Omissions ...

Three periods are used to indicate omissions from quotations.
Quotations must be reproduced word for word, letter for letter.
If letters or words within a sentence are to be omitted, indicate
with three dots . . .

If there is an omission after a complete sentence and the beginning of a following sentence, four dots are used . . . .

If there is omission of a paragraph or more, the omission is
indicated by a line of double-spaced periods extending the length
of the longest type-line of the quotation.

Quotation Marks "   "

Quotation marks are used in printing and writing to indicate
the beginning and ending of the exact words spoken or written.

Use quotation marks to enclose a direct quotation.

Example: The hold-up man said, "Reach!"

In reporting of conversation in dialogue, each separate speech

is enclosed in quotation marks. Every change of speaker is indicated by a new paragraph.

> *Example:* JONES said, "Don't sit in that chair."
> SMITH replied, "Why not?"

Use quotation marks to enclose slogans, mottoes, and slang
expressions.

A quotation within a quotation is indicated with single quotation marks.

> *Example:* "I was wrong," JONES said, "When I said,
> 'I saw the suspect.' "

When a quotation is interrupted, an extra set of quotation
marks is used. (See example immediately preceding.)

A question mark or exclamation mark is placed inside the
quotation mark when it is a part of the quotation; outside, if it
applies to the whole sentence. The period or comma is placed inside the quotation marks; the semicolon is placed outside.

> *Example:* He asked, "Were you there?"
> Did he say, "Wait for me"?
> He quoted from Shakespeare, "To be or not to be . . ."

Semicolon ;

A semicolon separates sentence elements with more distinctness than does a comma but with less distinctness than does a
period.

Use a semicolon between two independent clauses of a compound sentence when not joined by a conjunction (*and, but, or,
for*).

> *Example:* The road was impassable; we stopped.

Use a semicolon to separate clauses even if joined by con-
junctions if the clauses are long or contain commas within them-
selves.

Use a semicolon between clauses of a compound sentence
which are joined by such connectives as *therefore, hence, thus,
however, nevertheless, then, accordingly,* and the like.

> *Example:* SUBJECT was armed; therefore we took the necessary
> precautions.

Use a semicolon for clarity.

> *Example:* In the room were JONES, the victim; JANE, his wife;
> LILY SMITH, a friend of JANE'S.

Hyphen -

The hyphen is used as a connecting link between the syllables of a divided word or between compounded words.

A hyphen is used when it is necessary to divide a word at the end of a line of writing. The division should be made between syllables (pronounceable parts) only, and the hyphen placed at the end of the line. Never place the hyphen at the beginning of a new line.

A hyphen is used to connect words used as a single adjective.

Example: A door-to-door canvass was made.

He had an iron-clad alibi.

He works a five-day week.

A hyphen is used to compound numbers from twenty-one to ninety-nine.

New compounded words are hyphenated; when in doubt, consult a dictionary.

Errors in Composition

Errors in composition affect the logic of the report and hence will affect clarity and emphasis. More important errors to be avoided by the report writer include the following:

Comma Fault: Separating two sentences or independent clauses with a comma represents a common error.

Incorrect: The premises were entered, the officers conducted an intensive search for weapons.

Correct: The premises were entered. The officers conducted an intensive search for weapons.

Correct: The premises were entered, and the officers conducted an intensive search for weapons.

Correct: The premises were entered; the officers conducted an intensive search for weapons.

Sentence Fragment (See pp. 57-59.): Writing a fragment of a sentence as if it were complete represents a frequent error.

Incorrect: The SUBJECT ran for the rear door. When this officer entered the front door.

Correct: The SUBJECT ran for the rear door when this officer entered the front door. (The words *when this officer entered the front door* form what is called a dependent clause which is used as a modifier and requires the first part of the sentence to give it proper meaning.)

Incorrect: Peace officers prefer a revolver. Especially the .38 caliber.

Correct: Peace officers prefer a revolver, especially the .38 caliber. (*Especially the .38 caliber* is a modifying phrase dependent on the previous clause for meaning.)

Run-on Sentence Error: Failing to punctuate between independeit clauses or sentences is a common error.

Incorrect: The officers surrounded the building officer SMITH started for the rear door officer JONES covered the front door.

Correct: The officers surrounded the building. Officer SMITH started for the rear door. Officer JONES covered the front door.

Dangling Modifiers: Failure to express the noun or pronoun leaves the modifier with nothing to modify. A modifier is a word or group of words which changes or limits the meaning of another word.

Incorrect: On entering the building, the bullet holes are visible. (The phrase *on entering the building* has nothing to modify; the bullet holes did not do the entering.)

Correct: On entering the building, one can see the bullet holes. (The introductory phrase modifies *one*.)

Correct: When you enter the building, you can see the bullet holes.

•   •   •

In presenting the foregoing brief discussions about sentence structure, paragraphs, abbreviations, capitalization, numbers, pronouns, punctuation, some common punctuation errors, and errors in composition, the report writer has been exposed to some of the basic rules for writing. These rules are to the writer what tools are to the craftsman. Knowledge and observance of the rules of grammar and usage make for better report writing just as knowledge of tools and ability to use the tools make for better craftsmanship.

A report is made up of words, sentences, paragraphs. It is a narration by a person. Before one can narrate or tell anything he must have something to narrate. If there is something to narrate, it is essential that it be organized for presentation. Organization depends upon the purpose of the narration, upon who is going to read the report and for what reason, upon the use to which the report will be put, and upon the information possessed by the writer.

In preparing a report, the writer will ask himself: "What does the reader need to know? What does he need to know first? next? last?"

In checking the adequacy of the report, the writer will ask himself, "Have the WHO, WHAT, WHERE, WHEN, and HOW questions been answered accurately, completely, briefly, impartially? Is the report in good form?"

Mechanics of Composition in Investigative Report Writing

In the typing of investigation reports, particular ways of presenting the material are suggested here for the purpose of increasing the visual clarity of the report so that it can be read more easily and so that specific items of information can be located more readily. The basic idea behind any suggestion as to form and manner of presentation is to avoid ambiguity. There must be no question about the meaning of WHO, WHAT, WHERE, WHEN, and HOW.

Names. Names are the essentials of a report since the report is about individuals. Someone has to commit an offense. People are involved. People are identified by names. How the names are presented in the report is important. Identification numbers such as the military serial number or social security number can be considered to be a part of the name.

Spelling: Names must be spelled correctly—first, middle, and last. If the name of the individual is spelled more than one way, the different ways of spelling should be noted and their source explained. For example, a man's family may spell the son's name ELIOT SMYTH. The son may spell it ELLIOTT SMYTHE. There is no "correct" way to spell a proper name other than the way it is spelled by the person with that name.

Arrangement: In the report the last name or family name comes first, followed by a comma, then any title, then first and other names.

Capitals: All letters in the name are capitalized whenever the name appears in the report. When a title is used with a name, only the first letter of the title is capitalized.

Example: SMITH, Captain JOHN JOSEPH

Titles: Mr., Mrs., Miss may be treated as titles. Whether they are used in the report will depend upon whether they add to the clarity of the presentation.

Repetition: The first time the name of a person is introduced in the report it is written in full, all letters in capitals. Thereafter, the last name is sufficient unless there are others with the same or similar name with which there might be confusion.

Junior and Senior: These words are used when they are part of a person's name and and are treated as one would treat any title. They are usually abbreviated.

Example: SMITH, Jr., JOHN JOSEPH

SMITH, Sr., Capt., JOHN JOSEPH

Married Woman: A married woman's legal name is the last name of her husband followed by her own first name and middle name, if any. This is followed in parentheses by *Mrs.* with husband's first name and middle name or initial.

Example: SMITH, MARY ALICE (Mrs. JOHN JOSEPH)

After the first presentation of the name, it may be referred to as Mrs. SMITH.

Single Woman: A single woman's name is preceded by the title "Miss."

Example: Miss JONES, MARY DOROTHY

Unidentified Persons: When referring to a person whose name is unknown, refer to such person as "a man (or woman), name unknown, described as follows . . . " Do not refer to persons whose names are unknown as "John Doe," Jane Doe," or "Doe, name fictitious." If necessary, to avoid needless repetition of the description of such person or persons, he may be referred to as UNIDENTIFIED PERSON ONE, UNIDENTIFIED PERSON TWO, etc. At the first mention of such person reference is made as follows: UNIDENTIFIED PERSON ONE, a man, name unknown, described as follows . . .

Person Under Investigation: When referring to the person under investigation and there is only one such person, he may be referred to in the report either by last name or the word SUB-

JECT after the name has first been introduced in full. The two may be used interchangeably. However, if more than one person is under investigation, refer to the subjects by their last names only after the names have first been introduced in full.

Caution: Do not refer to persons under investigation as "the accused," "the defendant," "the suspect," and the like. Such references are improper in a report since they imply unwarranted judgment on the part of the investigator.

Firm Names: All firm names are written out in capital letters when first introduced. When frequent reference to a lengthy firm name may be required, it may be subsequently referred to by a shortened name or initials which are introduced with the first writing of the name.

Example: AMERICAN BITUMINOUS COAL AND
IRON AND RAG COMPANY (ABCIRC).

Agency Names: All agency names are written out in capital letters when first introduced. When frequent reference to an agency name may be required, it may be subsequently referred to by a shortened name or initials which are introduced with the first writing.

Example: CALIFORNIA YOUTH AUTHORITY (CYA)

Caution: Do not use initials when there are more than two firm names or agencies named in the report. Such practice may tend to confuse the reader.

Addresses. Addresses are important. They must be presented in full. They identify a location and there should be no possibility of confusion with any other location. If there is, the identification is inadequate.

Street and number, apartment number, room number or letter, or any other identification are a part of the addresses. There is but one address—a complete address.

Include city, postal zone, and state when first mentioned.

If a person's address is a military installation or ship, include (1) complete identification of particular unit to which he is assigned; (2) any barracks, building, or place which will facilitate in locating the person; (3) name of ship, owner, itinerary, etc.

Telephone Numbers. The telephone numbers at any given address may be considered as part of the address.

Telephone connections at any particular premises should be checked for the telephone number and address to which assigned at the telephone company. Make certain that a particular number is assigned to the particular address.

Indicate number of extensions, if any, with their numbers.

If the existence of a telephone on premises was not ascertained, so state.

If a telephone was located on the premises but no number was indicated, so state. Obtain number from the telephone company.

Dates. Write dates so there is no question as to the period identified by the writer.

When a single date is recorded, the name of the day precedes the date of the month, the month, and the year.

Example: Wednesday, 20 July 1960

When an inclusive period is recorded, the name of the day, the date of the month, name of the month of the first·day is written, and the name of the day, date of the month, name of the month, and year of the last day is written.

Example: Wednesday, 20 July—Wednesday,
3 August 1960
Wed., 20 July—Wed., 3 Aug. 60

When the inclusive dates cover two different years, the name, of the day, date of the month, name of the month, year of the beginning time and the name of the day, date of the month, name of the month, and year of the ending time are written as follows:

Example: Friday, 25 November 1960—Monday,
16 January 1961

Time. Although the twenty-four hour clock makes for the least possible confusion in indicating time, few civilian agencies use this method. The report writer should adhere to the method used locally.

Time is written in numerals. The hours are separated from the minutes by a colon and followed by the abbreviation a.m. (ante meridiem) and p.m. (post meridiem). Our word *meridian* comes from this and refers to midday or noon. On the twelve-hour clock all time is recorded before midday and after midday. Therefore it is necessary that a.m. or p.m. be used.

Examples: 12:01 P.M. (one minute after noon)
　　　　　12:01 A.M. (one minute after midnight)
　　　　　3:30 p.m.
　　　　　3:30 a.m.

With the twenty-four hour clock, time begins one minute after midnight and concludes with the following midnight. There are four numerals to designate any of the twenty-four hours.

Examples: 0001 hours((12:01 a.m.)
　　　　　0010 hours (12:10 a.m.)
　　　　　0100 hours (1:00 a.m.)
　　　　　1000 hours (10:00 a.m.)
　　　　　1500 hours (3:00 p.m.)
　　　　　2400 hours (12:00 midnight)

Inclusive periods of time may be indicated as illustrated in the following:

Examples: 2:30 a.m. — 5:30 a.m., Wed., 20 July 60
　　　　　0230 — 0530 hours, Wed., 20 July 60
　　　　　2:30 a.m. — 6:00 p.m., Wed., 20 July 60
　　　　　0230 — 1800 hours, Wed., 20 July 60
　　　　　2:30 a.m., Wed., 20 July 60 — 5:30 p.m., Thurs.,
　　　　　　21 July 60
　　　　　0230 hours, Wed., 20 July 60 — 1730 hours, Thurs.,
　　　　　　21 July 60

Witnesses. Witnesses are recorded in the manner as described under the heading *Names* discussed previously.

Give complete name, all letters capitalized; include identification numbers when pertinent.

Give complete address, residence and business, including telephone numbers.

Give other necessary identifying characteristics such as sex: male, female; race: white, black, yellow; nationality: American, French, English, Chinese, etc.; ethnic group: Mexican, Italian, Norwegian, etc. (See pp. 10-14.) Race refers basically to skin color; nationality refers to country of origin, a geographical area; ethnic group refers to nationality background of parents, cultural heritage. Be exact in your description. For example, a person is not Italian who is born in the United States of America. He is American by nationality and his ethnic background is Italian if his parents or grandparents were born in Italy.

Persons Who Are Sources of Information. When any information is obtained from a person, his name, title, business and residence addresses are included in the opening paragraph which introduces the information obtained.

> *Example:* SMITH, JOHN JOSEPH, General Manager, Retail Credit Bureau, 1476 XYZ Blvd., Denver, Colorado, was interviewed (visited, interrogated, examined, as the situation might be) on Wednesday, 20 July 1960, at his home, 6330 Ventura Blvd., Denver, Colorado, between 8:30 p.m. and 9:39 p.m. He stated that . . .

Records Which Are Sources of Information. When any information is included in the report which is obtained from records of any sort, reproductions (photostats, certified copies, etc.) of the original should be obtained and attached as an exhibit to the report. In introducing such information in the body of the report, the source of the record will be identified fully, including name of person in charge of the record as well as the record itself.

> *Example:* The records of the RETAIL CREDIT BUREAU, 1476 XYZ Blvd., Denver, Colorado, were inspected by Officer JONES on Thursday, 21 July 1960 between the hours of 8:30 a.m. and 11:30 a.m., copies of which are attached to this report as Exhibit B. SMITH, JOHN JOSEPH, General Manager, is in charge of the records. The records reveal that. . .

4

WHAT ARE THE PARTS OF THE REPORT?

ALTHOUGH THE narrative report will vary in its form from department to department, there are certain parts or elements that are common. This book makes no attempt to recommend any particular form. Discussion will be directed at certain parts or elements that are common to most narrative reports.

TITLE PAGE

The opening page of the narrative report may be a special page called the Title Page or something similar. This page will contain information about the investigation that prepares the reader for the contents of the report. Its purpose is to give the reader a chance to get a bird's-eye view of the report from glancing over a single page.

The Title Page or introductory page may be set up with a number of headings or items which identify particular sections marked off for specific information. There is no reason other than utility for the inclusion of headings or items. The number of items will vary from department to department. Following is an explanation of some items or headings which may be included on the title or introductory page.

File number. The file number of a case is a shorthand or abbreviated device used to classify the investigation. The kind of number system used is designated by the department and may take various forms. A hyphenated form is commonly used. The numbers may refer to the specific unit making the investigation, the name of the offense, and the number of the case.

This type of numbering system identifies the report as to its source (bureau, unit, section, division); the classification of the offense (murder, rape, burglary, robbery, etc.); and the sequential number of the case in the particular classification of offense.

For the purpose of illustration, let us assume that the homicide unit has been designated arbitrarily as 7; murder, a form of homicide, is statute number 187 in the penal code; and that the investigation is the thirteenth murder in the current year. The file number would be 7-187-13. Anyone familiar with the department numbering system would immediately know upon looking at this number that the report was prepared by someone in the homicide bureau, that it was a murder case, and that it was the thirteenth such case in the current period.

Other numbers may be added. A particular department may want to include a number designating the year. This number may be placed first or last; for example, 60-7-187-13 or 7-187-13-60, the 60 referring to the year 1960.

A three unit hyphenated system seems to be preferable since it keeps the number fairly short. By adding another unit, such as the year, the file number seems to be getting out of hand.

Status. The item labeled Status refers to the condition of the case. Ordinarily an investigation is "pending" or "closed." Other terms may be used, but the fewer used, the less possibility of error in describing the status of a case. A case is "closed" when the investigation is completed and the subject identified, when the case is ordered closed by a superior, when the prosecuting agency refuses to prosecute, when the subject is tried, when the subject dies, or whatever departmental policy sets out as a condition for "closed."

When a case is not "closed," it is "pending." There are just two categories of status. Either a case is "closed" in accordance with department regulations or it remains "pending." Sometimes the word "open" is used. If "open" is used, it must be defined. Usually "open" means "pending," and "pending" is a more expressive word. "Open" implies the question, Open to what? Prosecution? Further investigation? Delay?

Date of Report. The date of the report is the date on which the report is written. If more than one day is consumed in the writing of the report, the date of completion is used. If the report is dictated, the date of the report is the date of the completion of the dictation. The date of transcription from dictation or longhand is not the date of the report.

Report Made By. The report is made by all the investigators assigned to the case, and all are responsible for its construction and content. The responsibility for the investigation of the case is fixed by the signatures appearing under this heading. If another investigator worked on a phase of the case without having been assigned to the case, his name appears in the body of the report but not on the title page.

Period of Investigation. The period of investigation covers the actual period of time of the investigation described in the report. The beginning of the investigation is the date the investigators are assigned and begin to work on the case. This may not coincide with the date of the offense or when the department was first notified.

> *Examples:* Thursday-Saturday, 21-23 July 1960
> Wednesday, 20, Saturday, 23, Wednesday-Friday, 27-29 July 1960
> Wednesday, 20 July 1960, 9:30 a.m.-2:30 p.m.

In the first example, the investigation began on 21 July and was concluded on 23 July, 1960, and represents the period of time covered in the report. The second example indicates that the investigation was conducted on 20, 23, 27, 28, 29 July, and these dates were the period covered by the report. The third example shows that the investigation covered the hours noted of the particular day.

Names. This item lists the names, aliases, and addresses of all persons whose names appear in the report followed by such classification as witness, victim, informant.

Subject. This item identifies the person(s) by name, alias, address, who is discovered to be or may be a participant in the offense.

Until the identity of the perpetrator(s) is discovered, the item will contain the words UNIDENTIFIED PERSON, or UNIDENTIFIED PERSON ONE, UNIDENTIFIED PERSON TWO, depending upon how many persons the investigator believes to be involved in the offense.

When this item contains no name of an identified person, it may be advisable to list the name and address of the victim, or the name and location of the object of the offense, or the location of the offense.

If it is the policy of the department that the investigators submit initial and periodic reports during the course of the investigation, the initial report will contain the list of subjects with addresses and aliases. Subsequent reports will show the name of the principal subject followed by the phrase "and others."

Whenever additional subjects, aliases, and addresses are discovered, the word CORRECTION is written under this heading and the new names, aliases, and addresses are added. The explanation of the correction is made in the first paragraph of the *Details* section in the body of the report.

Offense. This item contains the offense or crime basic to the investigation. When more than one offense is involved, the more important one is placed first and capitalized. Underneath in lower case letters will appear the lesser offenses.

Synopsis. This is a single paragraph, if possible, which sums up the details of the report, indicates the action taken, and the results obtained. It is the investigation in a nutshell. It is the essence of the investigation as it was developed in the *Details* section of the report.

The purpose of the synopsis is to give the reader a general idea of the scope of the case and the answers to the questions: WHO, WHAT, WHEN, WHERE, HOW as briefly as possible.

To prepare a synopsis requires effort. The whole case must be reviewed from start to finish. The most essential elements are selected and brief notes made of them. From these notes, the essence of the case is briefly and clearly set forth. The synopsis is similar to the first paragraph of a news story which tells what the story is about in skeleton form.

The synopsis is not an outline of the investigation; it is a summary of the investigation. The synopsis may begin with such statements as:

Investigation revealed that. . .
Interview with JOHN SMITH disclosed that. . . .
Inspection of the records of the county clerk disclosed that. . .

The opening statement in the foregoing illustrations indicates the action taken, and should be followed by the results obtained.

The Title Page with the headings or items discussed above—

file number, status, date of report, report made by, period of investigation, names, subject, offense, and synopsis—enable the reader to get an accurate overall word picture of the particular investigation as narrated in the report. Some of the items may be omitted; others may be added. It is the opinion of this writer that those indicated are essential.

DETAILS

The section of the report headed Details is the body of the report and is the narration of the work done on the case. It embodies the questions which guided the investigation:

WHO is involved?
WHAT happened?
WHEN did it happen?
WHERE did it happen?
HOW did it happen?
(and perhaps, WHY did it happen?)

The writer of the report must always bear in mind that the primary purpose of his writing is to inform a reader—a reader who is assumed to know nothing about the case, nothing about the investigator, and nothing about any persons or things involved. In other words, the report writer is trying to present to the reader a problem and its solution, just as the investigator saw it and acted on it. The reader cannot be expected to add or fill in anything omitted. Nothing is left to the imagination of the reader about what the investigator did and discovered.

The section on the details of the investigation embodies the cardinal principles of good report writing: accuracy, completeness, brevity, impartiality, and form. (See pp. 33-66.) The information obtained and the sources of that information are enumerated in this section.

The first paragraph of the Details section usually presents the basis for the investigation, the reason for it, the information upon which it is predicated. This is set forth briefly. As suggested previously, when there are several reports about an investigation, the basis for the investigation appears in the initial report. In subsequent reports the first paragraph is used to discuss any corrections of previous reports.

The second paragraph in the Details section usually indicates the authority upon which the investigation is made. This may be one sentence naming the superior officer who directed that the investigation be made and who assigned the officer(s) to the case. The information contained in the first two paragraphs as discussed above does not appear in the *Synopsis*. (See p. 70.)

Subsequent paragraphs in the Details section relate the activities of the investigators during the investigation. The activities of the investigator are written in the order of time in which they were engaged. Experience has shown that a narrative chronologically developed makes a more readable and more readily understandable report.

Careful paragraphing clarifies each item of information spatially. (See pp. 41-42.) Numbering paragraphs permits reference to paragraph numbers in subsequent portions of the report.

Abbreviations should be used carefully. Whenever there is the slightest possibility of misinterpretation, do not abbreviate. (See p. 51.)

In summary, the Details of a report relate what was done by the investigators, what was found, who was contacted, and what information was obtained.

UNDEVELOPED LEADS

This section of the report follows the Details and sets forth all uncontacted sources of possible information. These uncontacted sources of possible information may have been developed during the investigation and for some reason had not been checked out. They may be leads that the investigator could not follow through. He may have thought them unimportant or unnecessary. Whatever the situation, this section gives the investigator an opportunity to inform the reviewer what sources were considered but not followed through and the reason.

The Undeveloped Leads section also provides the investigator with an opportunity to present possible sources of information that would have to be contacted by other departments for reason of jurisdiction or policy.

Undeveloped leads must be set out clearly so that they can be identified on the basis of the information provided. They must contain enough information to permit someone else to locate the lead and to follow through. The investigation should indicate the possible nature of the information to be obtained from the lead. (See pp. 41-42.)

CONCLUSIONS

In the *Details* section of the report, the investigator set forth the facts discovered without comment. He made no judgments, no evaluations, no inferences, no implications. He merely recited what he did and what he discovered.

Since the investigator is the only person who had first-hand experience, who observed the scenes and talked with the subjects, some departments feel that he should be given an opportunity to say what he thinks about the case, and should be able to express opinions, conclusions, and recommendations.

Since opinions, conclusions, and recommendations are mental inferences (that is, they are arrived at as a result of thinking about a set of facts), they should be presented, if at all, in a special section of the report about which there can be no doubt that the statements constitute inferences and not facts. For this reason, the section is a separate part of the report.

Even though this section is labeled Conclusions, the investigator must show a basis for his opinions, conclusions, and recommendations. He must state clearly that this is his opinion based on these facts. For example, it may be that the investigator is of the opinion that a certain witness is a liar. In the *Details* section where the witness is quoted, the investigator cannot call him a liar. The investigator can only point out, if such is the case, that the testimony of this witness is contrary to the particular findings. He can, however, in the Conclusions, point out that not only was the statement of the witness at odds with the observable situation, but that the witness exhibited signs that might be interpreted as indicating deception, such as: sweating, swallowing, fidgeting, particular nervous twitchings, etc.

In this section the investigator can express his opinion about the reliability of the statements of witnesses and others. He can say whether or not in his opinion certain persons will make favorable or unfavorable impressions as witnesses. He can suggest that the surveillance of a certain person might prove worthwhile. He can suggest what other type of investigation may be more productive of results.

The investigator, having discovered the facts, analyzed the facts, written them in a report, may state in the Conclusions his opinion as to what further action should be taken. He may point out that the case is not strong enough for prosecution because of lack of sufficient evidence, lack of intent, or lack of some element of the crime. He may recommend prosecution. He may recommend remedial action of a situation or condition disclosed during the investigation.

Recommendation should be made only on the basis of explicit facts enumerated in the report and should be justified by these facts. Recommendations should be practical and feasible.

The investigator should not feel slighted or hurt if his opinions and conclusions are rejected and his recommendations not followed. Since many investigators feel slighted when their inferences are not accepted, many departments have eliminated this section from the investigation report. However, the inferences of an investigator can be of help to the reviewer, providing the investigator does not expect his opinions to determine further action on the case.

The investigator must not use the words "innocent" or "guilty" in this or any other part of the report. The concepts of innocence and guilt are judicial judgments and have no place in investigative report writing. The investigator can say that in his opinion a person did or did not participate in a particular act and must support his opinion with the relevant findings stated in the report.

LIST OF WITNESSES

In the final report there will appear a list of witnesses. This list contains the names and addresses of those persons who have information about the case and who may be called upon to testify in a court action. Included with each name and address is a brief sentence indicating the nature of the information the person has. Reference should be made to the paragraph or page number in the *Details* section wherein mention is made of the witness and his information.

LIST OF EXHIBITS

The final section of the report is titled List of Exhibits. This list names the articles classified as exhibits—physical findings that may be introduced as evidence. Each must be adequately described and reference made to the paragraph or page number in the *Details* section in which initial mention is made of the exhibit. The location and custodian of the original of the exhibit must be indicated.

It is unusual for the original of an exhibit to be attached to a report since the original will be the material evidence gathered during the investigation of the case and its custody must be preserved. The original exhibits are placed in the care of an official custodian and safeguarded. For this reason, photostatic copies, photographs, or other reproductions constitute the exhibits listed in this section of the report.

Each exhibit listed is lettered or numbered for identification and reference purposes. The reproductions are attached to the report.

Exhibits are identified by letters of the alphabet or Roman numerals, such as Exhibit A, Exhibit B, or Exhibit I, II, etc. The order of listing of exhibits in this section of the report is determined by the order of presentation or reference to the exhibit in the *Details* section of the report. The exhibit is described, located geographically, and the paragraph or page number of the *Details* section in which the item is first mentioned is indicated in parentheses.

Examples: Exhibit A. Copy of statement of JOHN JONES relating his observation of behavior of JACK SMITH (3). Original statement in custody of property clerk.

Exhibit B. Photographic copy of registration certificate of ownership of vehicle reported stolen (7). Certified copy of certificate in custody of property clerk.

Exhibit C. Copy of report of Officer WHITTLE about recovery of vehicle (8). Original report in custody of evidence clerk.

Exhibit K. Photograph, front view, Plymouth, 2-door sedan, model P-21, green, license number (Calif.) ABC 098, engine number 472 096 631 (21). Vehicle in possession of owner, OSCAR GEORGE, 218 Ninth Street, City, California.

5

SUMMARY

Investigation report writing is a skill that can be developed through knowledge and practice. An investigator's ability will be measured by the report he writes because his report reflects the manner in which he conducted the investigation. A report should include negative findings as well as positive findings. The negative findings are as valuable as positive findings to evaluate what has been done as well as what should be done.

The investigator cannot depend upon a stenographer to do his reporting for him. If he does, the report will be a stenographer's report rather than an investigator's report. Further, a glib report will not conceal an inadequate and incomplete investigation. Identifying an offender without gathering the evidence necessary for judicial action cannot be the basis for a good report.

The investigator must be aware of the fact that practice alone is inadequate. One may practice errors until he becomes perfect in making errors. Experience, which is a form of practice, is an important ingredient in one's personal and professional development. But experience needs to be evaluated continually in the light of new knowledge and new ways of doing things. It is easy to rationalize old ways and to condemn new ways. When condemnation of the new or different becomes automatic, self-examination becomes essential. The investigator must become aware of his judgment. He must constantly ask himself, "Is my judgment in keeping with the immediate facts or is it a carry-over of a previous conclusion?" "Is my judgment based on the observable realities or on my feelings?"

Feelings are important. But they should act as motivants for digging out the facts rather than as bases for judgment.

The investigator performs an essential function in our society. How he performs this function is important to our society.

In attempting to summarize this monograph, a list of DO'S and DON'TS is presented as a stimulus:

DO'S:

DO know yourself.

DO analyze your problem.

DO know your job.

Know what you should do.

Let your observations determine the facts.

Know the difference between fact, hearsay, opinion, and conclusion.

Know how to write accurately.

Know the elements of grammar and composition.

Know the definitions of words.

Know when your words make sense.

Know when your words make nonsense.

DO obey the law.

DON'TS:

DON'T kid yourself.

DON'T let the report substitute for an investigation.

DON'T let your feelings determine the facts.

DON'T confuse fact with hearsay.

DON'T confuse fact with opinion.

DON'T confuse fact with conclusion.

DON'T assume the report is unimportant.

DON'T assume that arresting a suspect is equivalent to hav-having a case.

DON'T assume the function of the judiciary.

DON'T violate the law.

An investigator functions under the executive branch of our government. Upon assuming his office he swears to uphold the laws of the land. In order to uphold the laws of the land, he must perform his duties under these laws. When an investigator sets himself above or beyond the law, he violates the law he has sworn to uphold. No nation can long endure when lawless law-enforcement becomes prevalent.

APPENDIX

THE EXAMPLES of narrative reports included in this section are presented merely as illustrations and not as models. These examples do not necessarily reflect the practices suggested in the text, but reflect the practices of the departments for which they were written.

Interview and Investigation   *Accident Number*
      Summary   *2022-6-61-45*

FACTS

Received call at 1910 hours. Arrived at scene at 1921 hours. Accident occurred on US 40, 325 feet east of Donnor Lake gate. U.S. 40 is an east and west highway, straight and level at the accident scene. Roadway has two 11-foot asphaltic concrete lanes with a 5-foot improved shoulder and a 10-foot unimproved shoulder bordering each lane.

Vehicle No. 1 (THOMAS C. BLANK), a 1958 red Dodge Tudor sedan headed southwest, right front 22 feet south of the white line and the right rear 18 feet south of the white line. Right front locked wheel skid begins in east bound lane 350 feet east of Donner Lake gate, 2 feet south of the white line and runs for 129 feet to south shoulder, crosses improved south shoulder in an arc for 15 feet and continues on unimproved south shoulder for 16 feet ending under right front wheel. Right rear locked wheel skid marks begin in east bound lane 354 feet east of Donner Lake gate, 2 feet, 6 inches south of the white line and run for 123 feet to south shoulder, cross improved south shoulder in an arc for 15 feet and continue on unimproved shoulder for 6 feet ending under right rear wheel. Locked wheel skid marks from left front wheel begin 350 feet east at Donner Lake gate, 7 feet south of the white line and run for 45 feet to south shoulder, cross south improved shoulder in an arc for 12 feet and continue on unimproved shoulder for 103 feet ending under left front wheel. Left rear locked wheel skid mark begins 352 feet east of Donnor Lake gate, 7 feet 6 inches south of the white line and runs for 42 feet to south improved shoulder, crosses shoulder in an arc for 12 feet and continues for 90 feet on unimproved shoulder ending under left front wheel. Vehicle No. 1 RF fender and grill severely damaged.

Vehicle No. 2 (LEO P. DASH), a 1959 white Ford Tudor sedan, California license, headed northwest, left front wheel 5 feet north of the white line, left rear wheel 3 feet north of the white line. Side skid marks from left front wheel begin 325 feet east of Donner Lake gate, 3 feet south of the while line and run in an arc for 10 feet ending under left front wheel. Side skid marks from right front wheel begin 320 feet east or Donner Lake gate, 2 feet north of white line and run in an arc for 8 feet ending under right front wheel. No skid marks visible from rear wheels. Vehicle No. 2 severely damaged on left front door and the rear of the left front fender and windshield. Debris, water, headlamp glass found in east bound lane from white line to south shoulder 325 feet east of Donnor Lake gate.

STATEMENTS

Driver of vehicle No. 1 (BLANK) stated that he was west bound on U.S. 40 traveling approximately 45 to 50 mph, and that as he approached Donner Lake gate, he came up behind a large van type truck which was slowing down. The stop lamps on the truck were on, but no turn signal was visible, so he pulled into east bound lane to pass truck. As he drew abreast of the front end of the trailer, he saw vehicle No. 2 suddenly make a left hand turn into the entrance to Donner Lake. He applied his brakes, but was unable to stop or turn before he struck vehicle No. 2 in the left side.

Driver No. 2 (DASH) stated he was west bound on U.S. 40, and that as he approached the entrance to Donner Lake, he turned on his electrical turn indicators and began to slow down so that he could make a left hand turn. He checked his rear vision mirror, saw a truck behind and put out his arm to indicate he was preparing to turn left. The truck immediately behind him slowed, and he started his turn and was hit in the left side by vehicle No. 1.

Witness No. 1, GEORGE M. STOP, driver for All United Freight Lines, stated he was traveling west on U. S. 40 about 40 mph when he saw the left rear turn indicator begin to flash on the white Ford (vehicle No. 2). The Ford (vehicle No. 2) began to slow down and the driver put his arm out of the left window signalling for a left turn. He (witness No. 1) then applied the brakes on his trailer and began to slow down. At that time he looked into his rear view mirror and saw a red car approaching about 300 feet behind his trailer. The Ford and the truck continued to slow down for another couple hundred feet, and as the Ford started to turn, he saw the red car along side the trailer. The two vehicles came together in the east bound lanes and the Ford spun around into the west bound lane.

OPINIONS AND CONCLUSIONS

The physical evidence at the scene indicates that vehicle No. 1 passed the truck (witness No. 1) and struck the left side of vehicle No. 2 while vehicle No. 2 was attempting a legal left hand turn into the entrance to Donner Lake Park. Debris and glass in east bound lane and abrupt change of direction of skid marks from vehicle No. 2 indicate the point of impact as in the east bound lane approximately 325 feet east of Donner Lake gate. Complaint signed and citation issued for Driver No. 1's failure to pass safely to the left of the overtaken vehicle.

RECOMMENDATIONS

None.

4 photos by CHP
Notified of Accident 6/12/61
   Time: 1910
Investigated by Ledform 243
          Gowshee 325

Investigation Time: from 1921
  to 2005
Report typed 6/13/61 by C. S.

```
        CC: Constable, Clovis Area
FORM 1-1 CC: Burglary Detail, FPD                          60-38260;  60-38110;
        CC: Burglary Detail,      OFFICE OF THE SHERIFF    61-490;    61-1170
            Visalia P.D.
```

REPORTING DIVISION	FOLLOW UP REPORT		CASE NO.
PATROL			61-1720

CRIME CLASSIFICATION			DATE
P.C. 459 (SAFE BURGLARY)			13 Feb. 61

NAME OF VICTIM	ADDRESS	PHONE
PIPKIN & ASSOCIATES HARDWARE	7773 S. Clovis Ave., Fresno	AX 9-4031

SUSPECTS		ADDRESS	PHONE
	1 Robert Edward LEE (21)	7437 S. Helm, Fresno	N/P
	2		
	3		

PERSONS INTERVIEWED		ADDRESS	PHONE
	1		
	2		
	3		

PERSONS ARRESTED
Robert Edward LEE - Booking #9181

SYNOPSIS: This report concerns the Burglary and Safe Peel at PIPKIN & ASSOCIATES HARDWARE, 13 Feb. 61, 6:10 A.M.

While on routine patrol, the undersigned with several other units was dispatched by radio to PIPKIN & ASSOCIATES HARDWARE where the silent burglar alarm had been activated at 6:11 A.M. The undersigned with Deputy STARK in a separate unit, arrived 6:17 A.M. It was found that the front door had been jimmied, and the suspect was observed inside the office area working on the safe. WORSTEIN and STARK entered through the front door and were within 15′ of the office before SUSPECT was aware of their presence. SUSPECT dropped his tools and fled through the rear door. SUSPECT was ordered to stop; he kept running; a shot was fired over his head as he passed through the door. WORSTEIN chased SUSPECT to the rear of the fenced premises and captured SUSPECT who was hiding under a forklift truck. SUSPECT was placed under arrest, searched, and handcuffed. In searching SUSPECT, an 8″ screwdriver and a yellow handled pocket knife were found in his right front pocket. SUSPECT was wearing black leather gloves when arrested.

SUSPECT transported to County Jail and booked 836 P. C. Burglary.

CASE DECLARED CLOSED	☐ UNFOUNDED ☐ BY ARREST ☐ CONTINUED	☐ D. A. DENIED COMPLAINT ☐ COMPLAINT REFUSED BY VICTIM	INVESTIGATING OFFICER(S) BY B. Worstein #33, J. Stark #77

```
CC: Constable, Clovis District                60-38260;  60-38110;
CC: Burglary Detail, Fresno Police Department  61-490;    61-1170
CC: Burglary Detail,           OFFICE OF THE SHERIFF
    Visalia Police Dept.
```

REPORTING DIVISION PATROL	FOLLOW UP REPORT	CASE NO. 61-1720

CRIME CLASSIFICATION P.C. 459 (SAFE)		DATE 13 Feb. 61

NAME OF VICTIM	ADDRESS	PHONE
PIPKIN & ASSOCIATES HARDWARE	7773 S. Clovis Ave.,Fresno	AX 9-4031

		ADDRESS	PHONE
SUSPECTS	1 Robert Edward LEE (21)	7437 S. Helm, Fresno	None
	2	ADDRESS	PHONE
	3	ADDRESS	PHONE

		ADDRESS	PHONE
PERSONS INTERVIEWED	1 Suspect		
	2 Mrs. Marvin HAROLD	9474 S. Platt St., Fresno	CL 8-2245
	3	ADDRESS	PHONE

PERSONS ARRESTED Robert Edward LEE - Booking #9181

SYNOPSIS: This report pertains to the recovery of loot from a series of County, City and out of County Burglaries committed by suspect over a 60-day period.

At approximately 11:15 A.M. this date SUSPECT was transported to his residence near Clovis by the Clovis Constable, Deputies Worstein, Stark, and the undersigned. SUSPECT assisted in recovering the following described property:

(1) 1—Motorola, Stereo Hi-Fi, brown with orange trim, Serial #3733A, property of Mooney's, Visalia ....$ 134.95

(2) 1 — Zenith 19" portable T.V., light yellow, brown trim, Serial #5865641, property of Frank's Radio, Visalia 249.60

(3) 1 — Zenith 19" Portable T.V., brown and tan in color, Serial #3763261, property of Frank's Radio, Visalia 279.00

(4) 1 — Sony "Sterecorder" tape recorder, grey in color, Serial #12251, property of Frank's Radio, Visalia 399.00

(5) 1 — Zenith Transistor AM/FM Radio, portable, black, with chrome trim, Serial #4230258, Frank's Radio, Visalia 189.00

(6) 1 — Zenith Transistor, clock radio, Royal 850, salmon and cream, Serial #710285, property of Frank's Radio, Visalia 60.50

(7) 1 — Zenith Transistor Radio, Model #275,
Serial #546825, property of Frank's Radio,
Visalia 35.00
(8) 1 — Zenith Transistor Radio, Royal 100, light
grey, Serial #137022-A, property of Frank's
Radio, Visalia 27.00
(9) 1 — Zenith Transistor Radio, Royal 250, black,
Serial #983254-X, property of Frank's Radio, Visalia 27.00
(10) 1 — Zenith Transistor Radio, Royal 250, tan,
Serial #525857-X, property of Frank's Radio, Visalia 27.00
(11) 1 — 8 MM Mansfield movie camera, 1 Mansfield 8 MM projector; 1 Movie screen 30x40;
1 pistol grip movie camera attachment, grey
in color 100.00
(12) 1 — 30-06 Remington "Woodmaster" Rifle,
Model #740, Serial #277291, property of
Bob's Hardware, Fresno (Fresno P.D. Case)   103.75
(13) 1 — Benjamin .22 cal. Pellet gun, Model No.
312, Serial #639941-H, property of Bob's
Hardware, (Fresno P.D. Case) 16.65

Sub Total $2,248.45

The above described property was transported into the
Sheriff's Office, listed, and photographed this date. The property
belonging to the Visalia victims was turned over to Lt. ROBERT
HAMM, Visalia Police Department, this date.

The property belonging to BOB'S HARDWARE, Fresno, was
turned over to the Detective Division of Fresno Police Department, Lt. GEORGE GEORGES.

At approximately 12:20 P.M., 13 Feb. 1961, Mrs. MARVIN
HAROLD was contacted at her residence, 9474 South Platt
Street, Fresno. Mrs. Harold turned over the following described
property that had been sold to her husband by SUSPECT:

(1) 1 — Motorola Portable T.V. 17″, brown metal
case, Serial #39505-D, property of Mooney's,
Visalia .... $ 190.00
(2) 1 — Motorola Stereo, portable, brown with

orange trim, R15SF, Serial #5342, property
of Mooney's, Visalia 79.95

(3) 2 — Zenith Transistor Radios, Royal 50, white
and grey, Serial #521325-A and Serial #521326-
A, property of Frank's Radio, Visala @ 23.10
each 46.20

(4) 1 — Zenith Transistor Radio, Model 710, Serial
#269583-A, property of Frank's Radio, Visalia 41.40

Sub Total .... $ 357.55

The above property was turned over to the Visalia Police
Department this date. SUSPECT'S employer was contacted. The
following described articles were found hidden over a cooler in
the men's toilet:

(1) 1 — Ruger .22 cal. "Single Six" Revolver, Serial
#169951 (taken from Fresno Farmer Hard-
ware) 47.60

(2) 6—Boxes .22 cal. Ammo (Fresno Farmer Hardware) @ .70 ea. 4.20

(3) 1—Green plastic toolbox (Fresno Farmer Hardware) 5.00

Sub Total .... $ 56.80

This property was turned over to the Detective Bureau,
Fresno Police Department. A Visalia Burglary Detail arrived at
this office at approximately 2:00 P.M., 13 February 1961 and
furnished the undersigned with crime reports covering the
MOONEY'S FURNITURE and FRANK'S T.V. burglaries. In
checking the MOONEY loss, it was noticed that some Samsonite
Luggage, a portable typewriter, and an electric shaver, along
with the radios and televisions were listed as stolen. During the
first trip to SUSPECT'S home, articles fitting these descriptions were observed, but SUSPECT had stated the articles be-
longed to him and that they were not stolen. The Clovis Constable was contacted by phone. He returned to the SUSPECT'S
residence at approximately 6:00 P.M., 13 February 1961, and
picked up the following described property:

(1) 1 — Remington Typewriter, portable, two tone
grey, Serial #QR-4294923 .... $ 175.00

(2) 1 — Remington electric razor, "Rollamatic" .. 40.00

(3) 1 — Piece Samsonite luggage, ladies' train case,
light brown 25.00

(4) 1 — Piece Samsonite luggage, ladies' ward-
robe, powder blue 35.00

Sub Total ....$ 275.00

This property was tagged and placed in the evidence room
in the basement.

The total value of the property recovered as of 9:00 P.M., 13
February 1961, amounts to $2,937.80. At the suggestion of the
District Attorney's Office, Dep. JOE LITTLE, the motor boat
and motorcycle were left at SUSPECT'S home and SUSPECT'S
wife was advised not to dispose of these articles:

(1) 1 — 14′ Runabout boat, brown, no registration or serial
number.

(2) 1 — Boat Trailer, 2 wheel, metal, California License L-
420784.

(3) 1 — Johnson "Seahorse," 25 HP, Model #41-41D4, Serial
#814989.

(4) 1 — "Dot" Motorcycle, black, California License 31884.

MARVIN HAROLD, 9474 South Platt, advised that he will
recover the radios that he sold for SUSPECT and bring them to
this office.

SUSPECT will be questioned further 14 February 1961.

IF ADDITIONAL SPACE IS REQUIRED USE CONT. REPORT, FORM 1-3

CASE	☐ UNFOUNDED	☐ D. A. DENIED COMPLAINT	INVESTIGATING OFFICER(S)
DECLARED	☐ CONTINUED	☐ COMPLAINT REFUSED	BY Sgt. Richard Bain #10
CLOSED	☐ BY ARREST	BY VICTIM	

11-29-61 mb   Sgt. R. Bain No. 10

FORM 1-1

```
CC: Constable, Clovis Area              60-38260;  60-38110;
CC: Burglary Detail, FPD                61-490;    61-1170
CC: Burglary Detail,    OFFICE OF THE SHERIFF
    Visalia PD
```

REPORTING DIVISION			CASE NO
PATROL		FOLLOW UP REPORT	61-1720

CRIME CLASSIFICATION			DATE
P.C. 459 (SAFE)			13 Feb. 61

NAME OF VICTIM		ADDRESS	PHONE
PIPKIN & ASSOCIATES HARDWARE		7773 S. Clovis Ave., Fresno	AX 9-4031

SUSPECTS		ADDRESS	PHONE
1	Robert Edward LEE (21)	7437 S. Helm, Fresno	N/P
2			
3			

PERSONS INTERVIEWED		ADDRESS	PHONE
1	Robert Edward LEE (21)	Fresno County Jail	
2	Betty LEE (20)	7437 S. Helm, Fresno	N/P
3			

PERSONS ARRESTED
Robert Edward LEE - Booking #9181

SYNOPSIS: This report pertains to a statement taken from a SUSPECT caught during commission of a safe burglary. SUSPECT admitted three prior burglaries at PIPKIN & ASSOCIATES HARDWARE; one other county burglary; five Fresno Police Department burglaries and two burglaries within the City of Visalia. Report also covers the recovery of a quantity of stolen property.

At approximately 8:50 A.M., 13 Feb. 61, a statement was taken from the SUSPECT at the Fresno County Jail by Deputy District Attorney HYMAN REESE in the presence of Sgts. R. BAIN and JAMES QUIST, Constable A. HARDY and Court Reporter HAROLD KOLLOP.

The first portion of the statement dealt with the burglary of PIPKIN & ASSOCIATES HARDWARE this date when SUSPECT was apprehended during its commission. SUSPECT gave the following story:

(1) SUSPECT LEE left his residence at 7437 So. Helm, Fresno, at approximately 5:45 A.M. on this date. He drove his 1949 Plymouth, California License GOK 923, to a point on Hammer Street, approximately 90′ South of Pomona Avenue, where he parked in front of 962 Hammer Street. He arrived there at approximately 6:00 P.M., removed a small screwdriver from his car, removed his shoes, put on an old pair of cowboy boots and walked easterly on Pomona about one block to the hardware store. SUSPECT

gained entry to the building by prying the front door located on the east side of the building with the screwdriver. Once inside SUSPECT walked directly to the rear door located on the south side of the building near the southwest corner and opened same. He stated this was for the purpose of having an escape route in the event someone came. SUSPECT then walked to a display shelf at northeast corner of the store and removed two pry bars, a screwdriver, a wedge, and a small handled sledge hammer. SUSPECT then started peeling the safe which was located in a large wooden cabinet between the cash register and previously unlocked rear door. This door leads into fenced backyard from a one room office. Peel job was started at the lower right corner. He was making fair progress, but the safe (on casters) kept moving out of its cubby hole. SUSPECT then pulled it out, rolled it down the hall to the office, tipped it on its back, and resumed prying. When these OFFICERS entered the front door, SUSPECT ran out the back door, then west through the yard to an open shed, where he attempted to hide from these OFFICERS. SUSPECT states his sole motive for the burglary was to obtain money. He knew where the safe was. When he left his residence, his wife, who is 7½ months pregnant, was sleeping and knew nothing of his plans. SUSPECT stated that this was his first burglary, and the only other time that he was in trouble was approximately 1½ years ago in Bay Town, Texas. He was employed by COAST OIL COMPANY at that time and reported a phony armed robbery, pocketed the money, and was caught for this offense.

After approximately five minutes of further questioning, SUSPECT broke down and agreed to relate all of his activities. He advised that he came to Fresno approximately one year ago from New Mexico, where he was employed by the SAFETY BURGLAR ALARM CO. He is presently buying his home and is employed by the A. T. HENRY COMPANY, 842 East Fulton Street, Fresno, as shop foreman.

SUSPECT states he has burglarized PIPKIN & ASSO-

CIATES HARDWARE on three other occasions and described these jobs as follows:

(2) The first burglary was approximately the Wednesday before New Year's Day (1961). (Our file #60-38110 shows 28 Dec. 60.) SUSPECT states he was driving his 1949 Plymouth sedan. He parked in the HARPER VILLAGE SHOPPING CENTER approximately three blocks south of PIPKIN & ASSOCIATES HARDWARE. He took a large screwdriver from his car and walked to the hardware store, where he arrived just in time to see victim, PIPKIN, drive away from his closed store. SUSPECT places the time between 7:00 P.M. and 8:00 P.M. SUSPECT states he walked to the west boundary of the rear lot near the northwest corner where he scaled a low section (6') of redwood fence. Inside, SUSPECT walked to the rear door (S.W. corner) which opens into the office and proceeded to pry this door at the lock. When the door was forced, SUSPECT entered the office, put on a pair of cotton gloves found in the office, walked to a counter which was located in a hallway back in northeast corner of the building, obtained pry bars on display, returned to the safe, and proceeded to peel same. SUSPECT states he removed approximately $250.00 in currency and change from safe, (VICTIM states $382.84), left the building and back yard at point of entry, keeping the cotton gloves which he found at the store. VICTIM's tools were also left at the scene.

(3) SUSPECT describes the second burglary of PIPIN & ASSOCIATES HARDWARE AS FOLLOWS:

SUSPECT drove his 1949 Plymouth to the scene, arriving between 7:00 P.M. and 8:00 P.M. (F.S.O. case 61-490 reported 4 Jan. 61 at 9:00 A.M.). SUSPECT parked his vehicle one block west of the store at approximately the same spot he parked this A.M. (Hammer Street). SUSPECT removed a screwdriver from his vehicle, climbed the rear fence at the same spot as before, and pried the same rear door as before. Inside, SUSPECT found a much smaller safe compared to the first burglary and stated, "It must have been a loaner—while they were repairing the original safe." SUSPECT states he was only interested in obtaining money. He obtained pry bars, etc. from the same display rack and wore the cotton gloves stolen in the first burglary. SUSPECT rolled the smaller safe out of the cabinet housing same (located in the hallway), then rolled it into the back office where he turned it on its side and proceeded to pry it open. He removed approximately $500.00 in currency and left the building and back yard by same route as when entry was made. He states the cotton gloves were left at the scene. SUSPECT returned to his vehicle and drove to TOWNE DRIVE-IN where he had a cup of coffee. At this point, SUSPECT was questioned as to what happened to the money from these first two jobs. He advised that he made house payments, paid on other bills, and purchased a Dog Motorcycle from HENRY A. WILLIAMS COMPANY, located on East Van Ness Avenue in Fresno. The purchase price of the cycle was $200.00. The motorcycle is presently at his residence in Clovis. SUSPECT states that he did not purchase anything for his home, or for his wife, except groceries. SUSPECT was asked if his wife was aware of his activities. He stated that she was not. He was then asked how he explained the extra money and he advised that in addition to his regular job, he had a job with VALLEY WIDE VACUUM CLEANER COMPANY of Fresno as a salesman and worked on a commission basis which his wife couldn't or didn't check. He states he held this job from 5 Nov. 60 to 15 Jan. 61. He worked nights during this period and sold approximately five cleaners for which he received $35.00 each. SUSPECT states at his regular job he receives $390.00 per month.

(4) SUSPECT states his third burglary at PIPKIN & ASSOCIATES HARDWARE was pulled approximately 9 Jan. 61 between 7:00 P.M. and 8:00 P.M. (F.S.O. case 61-1170 shows date as 9 Jan. 61). On this occasion, SUSPECT drove his 1949 Plymouth to a point 1 block north of the store (Kadota Ave.) where he parked in front of a vacant

house. He walked to the rear fence, but was afraid to climb the fence at the usual spot because a light in a house just west of this point lit up the area. Instead, he climbed the higher portion of the west fence at the approximate center of the lot. This put him on the roof of the sheds located along this fence. From here he dropped into the backyard. SUSPECT was wearing the same gloves he was wearing when caught this A.M., and used the same method of entry as before. When he got to the safe, he saw a note attached which read, "Safe Open." This he believed to be the original safe which had been repaired. He opened the unlocked safe, pried an inner compartment that was locked, but found no money. Inside the safe, however, he did find a key to the Coca Cola machine which stands beside the front door. With the help of the key and an Allen Wrench found in the store, he got into the vending machine. SUSPECT stated he thought the VICTIM may have hidden his money in the machine. When no money was found, SUSPECT left the scene by same means and route as before, returning to his car, and rode around a while before going home.

(5) SUSPECT then proceeded to give details of the first of five burglaries committed within the city limits of Fresno:

On approximately 15 Jan. 61, between 7:00 P.M. and 8:00 P.M. (F.P.D. case #L-11080 shows 11 Jan. 61), SUSPECT burglarized the FRESNO FARMER HARDWARE located at 4072 West Blackstone Avenue, Fresno. He gave the following details: SUSPECT drove his 1949 Plymouth to the parking lot at FOOD TOWN MARKET, located one block south of the hardware store, where he parked. He took a screwdriver, the same gloves he was caught with, and walked to the rear of the store where he climbed the fence. Entry was gained by prying a rear door. Inside, SUSPECT took a .22 cal. pistol from a display case; then proceeded to the office which is located on the mezzanine. He removed the pins from the safe hinges and pried the door with a pry-bar that he had obtained downstairs. The door was removed and SUSPECT took in excess of $900.00 in currency and change from the safe. (Victim reported $926.13.) From the downstairs section, SUSPECT took a green plastic tackle box, placed the money and the revolver in same, and left the store at the point of entry. He states the revolver and tacklebox are hidden at his place of employment. With part of the cash he purchased a 14' runabout boat, a boat trailer, and an outboard motor from PETE TOOMER, who works at the VALLEY WIDE VACUUM CLEANER COMPANY of Fresno. Purchase price of the complete outfit was $450.00. He then paid off a $307.00 note to HAPPY TIME FINANCE, 701 West Van Ness, a $75.00 utility bill, and a $51.00 optometrist bill to BETTER VISION, 657 Eye St.

(6) During January, 1961, SUSPECT states he burglarized HUNTER HARDWARE, located on 420 N. Olive Ave. (F.P.D. Case M-1700 - HUNTER SEED COMPANY, 420 North Olive reported 4 Jan. 61). The burglary occurred between 7:00 P.M. and 9:00 P.M. SUSPECT states that he parked his Plymouth beside the PURITY COMPANY, 408 N. Olive Ave., walked to the rear of the hardware store where he climbed a fence constructed of bamboo, wire and plastic venetian blinds. He walked through the section of the yard used as a nursery, broke the glass in a rear door, reached in, and unlocked the door from the inside. SUSPECT wearing the same gloves, placed a burlap sack found at the scene over the glass and smashed same with his gloved fist. Inside, SUSPECT could not locate the safe and left by same route as point of entry, taking nothing.

(7) Shortly after the first PIPKIN & ASSOCIATES HARDWARE burglary, SUSPECT states he burglarized BOB'S HARDWARE, located at Thorne & First Streets in Fresno. He was fairly certain it was on a Friday night and was between 7:00 P.M. and 9:00 P.M. (F.P.D. Case F-182030 - reported 31 Dec. 60).

Again, SUSPECT drove his 1949 Plymouth, parking same on Thorne or First, near the hardware store. He took a screwdriver and a Crescent Wrench from his car, walked to the rear of a dry goods store, located next to BOB'S HARDWARE where he climbed the fence. He then proceeded to the fence enclosing the backyard of the hardware store, which he described as "a high fence." With the Crescent Wrench, SUSPECT removed the bolts from the locking device on the fence gate and entered the backyard. SUSPECT attempted to pry a rear door with no success. He then tore some boards off what he thought was a window and found it was a cooler duct. This was found on the back wall of the building inside of an unlocked storage room. Inside of the duct, he ran into "some metal stripping", which he couldn't handle with the tools on hand. SUSPECT returned to his vehicle, drove to CROSE HARDWARE, Moroa and Shaw, purchased a pair of tin snips and returned to BOB'S HARDWARE. Here, he cut the metal stripping with the shears and entered the building through the duct. Inside, he found a floor safe and no attempt was made on it. He removed approximately $50.00 (VICTIM says $83.00) in silver from the cash register, a 30-06 automatic rifle from the gun case, also a .22 cal. pellet pistol, and three boxes of .22 cal. pellet ammunition. SUSPECT opened the back door from the inside, went through the open gate, climbed the fence, and returned to his vehicle.

(8) During January, 1961, SUSPECT states he burglarized SWEDE JOHANSON'S HARDWARE COMPANY at Herndon and Central Avenues in Fresno (F.S.O. Case 60-38260 reported 9:00 A.M., 30 Dec. 60). SUSPECT drove his 1949 Plymouth to the parking lot at CENTRAL LANES BOWL, where he parked same. He removed a screwdriver and the same black gloves from his vehicle, walked to the rear of JOHANSON'S HARDWARE, climbed a rear fence into the nursery area, and pried the rear door. Inside, SUSPECT found a floor safe, obtained pry bars from a display rack, and pried unsuccessfully on the safe for approximately one hour before leaving by way of entry, taking nothing.

(9) SUSPECT states that during the first two or three days in February, 1961, approximately 7:00 P.M. to 8:00 P.M. he again burglarized the FRESNO FARMER HARDWARE (F.P.D. case M-11080 reported 9:30 P.M., 12 Jan. 61). SUSPECT states he is not sure of this date, but recalls it was the same night that RIMSON & HAYWARD, several buildings away, was broken into. (SUSPECT formerly worked for R & H. Some friends still employed there told him about the R & H burglary and that the police thought the same man pulled both jobs.) He states he did not pull the R & H burglary. SUSPECT again drove the same vehicle, parked on the FOOD TOWN MARKET parking lot and used the same method of entry as used on the first job. SUSPECT states he spent three hours on a money search and got $12.00 or $13.00 from an olive drab metal box found near the gun case. This box was locked, but the key was in the lock. SUSPECT left by same means as before.

(10) SUSPECT states before Christmas, 1960 (latter part of November or first part of December), he burglarized MOONEY'S FURNITURE COMPANY of Visalia. This job was pulled between 7:00 P.M. and 9:00 P.M. (Visalia Police Department Case 71760, 5 Dec. 60). SUSPECT states he went to Visalia to contact several leads on possible prospects for vacuum cleaner sales. One of his appointments was cancelled. He parked his Plymouth in a parking lot near MOONEY'S, pried the rear door with a screwdriver, prybar, and a hammer, and entered the store. He first made a money search and found none. SUSPECT then removed the following described merchandise:

(a) Two used T.V. sets, portable, 17″ screens. One was a Hot Point, white with coral front. The other was an Olympia, same color. He states these were faulty, so he later took them apart, smashed up the pieces and hauled them to the dump.

(b) One new Motorola Portable Stereo, blue case with silver trim. This is at SUSPECT'S home.

(c) Approximately ten new Motorola and Tom Thumb

transistor radios. Someone later stole five of these from the back of his vehicle when it was unattended. Three, with dead batteries, were later thrown in the canal which crosses Peach Avenue, just south of Jensen, and one was sold to an employee of VALLEY WIDE VACUUM CLEANER COMPANY, named MABEL. This was a Motorola and he received $15.00 or $20.00 for same. (It was later found that this party sent the radio to a son in Florida for a Christmas present, but she is willing to pay VICTIM full price. Visalia Police Department was furnished her full name and will handle.) Another transistor was sold to a part time employee of VALLEY WIDE VACUUM CLEANER COMPANY, name unknown, who works in the shop and has a brother named STEVE, who is a full-time employee. Selling price was $20.00.

(d) 1 — 8 MM Mansfield Movie Camera, projector, screen, splicer, and carrying case. He recalled that the price tag on the complete outfit was $199.95. This set is at SUSPECT'S residence.

(e) 1 — New 17" or 19" Motorola Portable Television, brown plastic case. This was sold to MARVIN HAROLD, an employee at RIMSON and HAYWARD, where SUSPECT formerly worked, for $150.00.

(f) Two new smaller Motorola Portable Stereos, one green and brown, the other coral with gold flecks. The green and brown machine was also sold to MARVIN HAROLD for $50.00. The second stereo is supposedly torn down and is in the shop at his place of employment.

SUSPECT states that he piled the loot by the back door, making four or five trips, drove his car to the back door, loaded up and returned to Fresno. He told MARVIN HAROLD that he bought the articles at a good discount at a bankruptcy sale in San Francisco. (Victim estimated total loss at $1,099.70.)

(11) SUSPECT states from 7 to 14 days after the MOONEY job, he burglarized a television store located on

the east side of Mt. View Blvd. near the center of Visalia. This job was pulled between 7:00 P.M. and 9:00 P.M. (Visalia P. D. Case #72240 occurred 13 Dec. 60, victim: FRANK'S RADIO AND T.V.) SUSPECT couldn't recall the name of this store, but stated they specialized in Zenith Sales and Service. SUSPECT states he parked near the store on a side street and walked down the alley to the rear of the store. It was exceptionally foggy at the time. SUSPECT found ladder at the side of the building and used it to climb to the roof where he opened an unlocked skylight. He then pulled the ladder to the roof, stuck it down through the skylight opening, and entered the building. He first made a money search which netted approximately $45.00 from the cash register. The balance of the loot is described as follows:

(a) Two Zenith 19″ portable televisions, 1 brown, 1 yellow and brown. Both are at SUSPECT'S residence.

(b) From 10 to 14 Zenith transistor radios. Some are hidden at his home. MARVIN HAROLD sold 5 or 6 for SUSPECT for which SUSPECT gave him one transistor radio. He has not received the money for two of these from HAROLD. For two, he received $25.00 each and for one, he received $20.00.

(c) 1 — Sony Stereo tape recorder, portable, black and grey.

This is all that SUSPECT could recall. He states he departed by a side door, facing the alley, made three trips carrying loot to the end of the alley where he loaded it into his vehicle and returned to Fresno. Northbound on 99 at Jensen Avenue on the outskirts of Fresno, SUSPECT ran the stop light (due to the fog), and was stopped by a CHP Officer. He states he explained the merchandise by stating he was an appliance salesman.

(12) SUSPECT states on the night he burglarized the FRESNO FARMER HARDWARE, he also burglarized SUBURBAN HARDWARE, 911 E. Blackstone Avenue, Fresno. This job was pulled prior to the FRESNO FARMER job and occurred at approximately 6:00 P.M.

(Fresno P.D. Case L-6420). SUSPECT states that he parked his vehicle in a drive-in parking lot approximately one block south of the store. He took a small screwdriver, walked around the block, entered a dry irrigation ditch, and walked easterly up same to a point even with the rear fence. Here he raised the wire fence and crawled under. SUSPECT first tried to pry a rear door protected with two padlocks and failed. He pried another rear door that was nailed shut, using the screwdriver and a mop handle that was found at the scene. He recalled a lot of roofing paper stacked just inside the door. Inside, SUSPECT could not find a safe and the cash register was empty. He was there five to ten minutes, and upon leaving, took a large screwdriver and two smaller ones. These are in his toolbox at his place of employment. SUSPECT departed at point of entry.

This statement was compiled at approximately 11:00 A.M., 13 February 1961. At that time, the Fresno Police Department and Visalia Police Department were contacted and stated they would furnish this department with copies of their case reports.

Sgt. R. Bain #10

COMPLAINT REPORT

3884 No. First St., Fresno	Malicious Mischief	61-2573
−LOCATION−	−NATURE OF COMPLAINT−	−SERIAL NO.−
Barton BOHANAN	2771 East Tyler	AM 6-9278
−COMPLAINANT'S NAME−	−ADDRESS−	−PHONE−

McFADDEN	10:00 PM	18 Aug 61	DANA	Telephone
RECEIVED BY	TIME	DATE	OFFICERS ASSIGNED	HOW REPORTED

Complainant reports several juveniles broke large glass window at the R & R Cooling Company.

See Miscellaneous Report. Unable to contact victim at this time. Hold for follow up by Detectives.

VALUE $_____ RECOVERED $_____

APPROVED:_____   OFFICER McFADDEN

OFFICE OF THE SHERIFF

MISCELLANEOUS REPORT		CASE NO. 61-2573		
REPORTING DIVISION Patrol		LOCATION 3884 North First, Fresno, California		
CRIME CLASSIFICATION PC 594, Malicious Mischief				DATE 18 Aug 61
NAME OF VICTIM R & R COOLER COMPANY		ADDRESS 3884 North First, Fresno		PHONE AM 9-7892
REPORTED BY Barton BOHANAN		ADDRESS 2271 East Tyler, Fresno		PHONE AM 6-9278
RECEIVED BY McFADDEN		TIME 10:00 PM	DATE 18 Aug 61	VIA Telephone
SUSPECTS	1 Unknown	ADDRESS		PHONE
	2	ADDRESS		PHONE
PERSONS INTERVIEWED	1 BOHANAN	ADDRESS		PHONE
	2 See Details Below	ADDRESS		PHONE
PERSONS ARRESTED None...				

This investigation concerns damage inflicted by vandals on a large plate glass window of a business establishment. Victim unknown at this time.

Contacted BOHANAN who stated that at 10:00 P.M., this date, he observed 6 or 7 juvenile males loitering about the front of the R & R COOLING COMPANY, 3884 North First, Fresno, California. His attention was distracted momentarily, and he heard glass breaking. He looked back and observed the juveniles running from the area in an easterly direction. BOHANAN discovered that the large plate glass window in the front of the building was broken. He then reported the incident to this department.

Investigation disclosed that apparently two separate objects had been thrown at the window, breaking it.

A search was made of the immediate area for possible suspects. Observed three male juveniles walking near the corner of Dakota and Ashlan. During questioning, all three suspects stated they were returning home from the bus stop, and denied any knowledge or implication in the crime. All subjects released and directed home.

Subjects questioned are as follows:

Fred AVENT, WMJ, 13, 9429 East Harvey

James AVENT, WMJ, 15, 9429 East Harvey

Boice MEYERS, WMJ, 16, 9278 East Lewis

Unable to ascertain the owner of the building, or the proprietor of the business at this time. A sign on the door indicates business will be open at 9:00 A.M., Saturday, 19 Aug. 61.

No physical evidence found at the scene.

IF ADDITIONAL SPACE IS REQUIRED, USE CONTINUATION REPORT, FORM 1-3   INVESTIGATING OFFICER(S)

A. DANA, Depty #77

CRIME REPORT

SHERIFF'S OFFICE

				Case Number
Specific Offense		*Reporting Department*		61-2573
PC 594 MAL, MISCHIEF				

Date and time occurred, day of week	Location of occurrence	Division—Beat	Date and time reported to department
18 Aug 61 10:00 PM Fri.	3884 N. First, Fresno	Patrol 3	18 Aug 61 10:00 PM

Victim's name (firm name if business)	Residence address (business address if firm)	Residence phone	Business phone or address
Charles TOORAM	9122 E. Kings Canyon	CL 1-5640	AM 9-1168

Person reporting offense	Residence address	Residence phone	Business phone or address
Barton BOHANAN	2271 E. Tyler, Fresno	AM 6-9278	None

Person who discovered crime	Residence address	Residence phone	Business phone or address
BOHAN	Same	Same	None

WITNESS(ES): Name	Residence address	Residence phone	Business phone or address
Bohanan	Same	Same	None
Robert C. MILLER	922 Thesta, Fresno	BA 2-6643	AM 9-7892

Victim's occupation	race	sex	age	Type of premises or location where offense was committed
Sign Painter	W	M	62	Single story stucco, business, corner, unincorporated area.

CRIMES AGAINST PROPERTY	CRIMES AGAINST THE PERSON
Point where entrance was made: Not Applicable	**Weapon—Force or means used:**
Exact location of property when stolen Not Applicable	**Exact location of victim at time of offense**
Instrument used (describe) Hands, Possibly Rocks	**Victim's activity at time of offense**
Method used to gain entrance Not Applicable	**Exact words used by suspect**

Where were occupants at time of offense?
Business closed for day

Apparent motive—Type of property taken or obtained
To damage plate glass window

Trademark of suspect(s)—Actions or conversation
Throw objects against unattended store window, breaking same, flee scene

Vehicle used by suspect(s)—Year, make, body type, color, license number and any other identifying marks
Unknown

SUSPECT(S):

	Name	Address used	Hair	Eyes	Hgt.	Wgt.	Age	Identification Numbers (if any)
No. 1								
No. 2								
No. 3								

DETAILS: Describe evidence; summarize details not given above; itemize and describe any property obtained, including serial numbers and value—

Victim, TOORAM, states damaged building leased to R & R COOLER COMPANY, Robert C. MILLER, Proprietor. MILLER states business closed at 5:30 AM, 8-18-61 and window was not damaged. At 10:00 PM, 18 Aug 61, investigating officers arrived at scene in response to complaint from BOHANAN and discovered the front plate glass window 70" x 36", broken. BOHANAN states that prior to reporting, he observed 6 or 8 male juveniles loitering around front of building. He then heard glass break and observed juveniles running from scene.

No physical evidence found at crime scene.

Estimated damage to window $48.30

R. BAIN, Sgt. No. 10

19 Aug 61   10:00 AM

LIST CASE NUMBERS OF ANY OTHER OFFENSES CLEARED OR CONNECTED WITH THIS REPORT; USE ADDITIONAL SHEET IF NECESSARY			
APS number and date	Signature of reporting officer R. BAIN, Sgt #10	Badge or serial number 2305	Date and time report written 19 August 61 10:00 AM
Warrant Issued?	Signature of supervisor approving H. McKINNEY, Lieut #6	Badge or serial number 2303	Date and time report reviewed 19 August 61 1:00 PM

CC: Probation Office
FORM I-I CC: Juvenile Department
Fresno Sheriff's
Dept.

OFFICE OF THE SHERIFF

REPORTING DIVISION					CASE NO.
PATROL			FOLLOW UP REPORT		61-2573

CRIME CLASSIFICATION					DATE
P.C. 594					22 Aug 61

NAME OF VICTIM			ADDRESS	PHONE
Charles TOORAM			9122 E. Kings Canyon, Fresno	AM 9-1168

			ADDRESS	PHONE
SUSPECTS *	1	Howell GORDON (16)	9313 E. Lewis, Apt.A, Fresno	AM 7-4634
	2	Thomas HARKERSON (13)	9277 E. Lewis, Fresno	AM 4-3724
	3	Boice MEYERS (16)	9278 E. Lewis, Fresno	N/P

			ADDRESS	PHONE
PERSONS INTERVIEWED **	1	All Suspects		
	2	Fred AVENT (13)	9429 E. Harvey, Fresno	AD 5-0442
	3	Junior HARKERSON (15)	9277 E. Lewis, Fresno	AM 4-3724

PERSONS ARRESTED
Thomas HARKERSON Boice MEYERS Cited Juv. Bureau--GORDON booked Juv. Hall
* Susp. (4) James AVENT (15) 9429 E. Harvey, Fresno AD 5-0442
** PI (4) Buddy ALLEN (15) 9485 E. Tyler, Fresno N/P

SYNOPSIS: This report pertains to the investigation of a broken store window at 3884 North First Street, Fresno, California, reported 18 Aug. 61.

A miscellaneous report was prepared by Deputy DANA, 18 Aug. 61, to cover this complaint as the patrolman was unable to obtain the information for a crime report due to the late hour. This report mentioned that Fred AVENT, James AVENT, and Boice MEYERS were found near the crime scene by the officer, were questioned, denied knowledge of the vandalism, and were sent home.

Boice MEYERS was contacted at his home by the undersigned at approximately 9:30 A.M., 22 Aug. 61, and was interviewed in the presence of his mother. MEYERS at first denied any knowledge of the broken window, but later admitted that on Friday, 18 Aug. 61, at approximately 10:00 P.M., he was with a group of friends, enroute home from the playground at First and Harvey and passed by the store that was reported damaged. MEYERS stated that as he turned east on Lewis from First, he heard the sound of breaking glass, but he had no idea what had happened and was sure that the responsible party was not in his group. MEYERS identified his group as follows:

(1) (2) Thomas and Junior HARKERSON, 9277 E. Lewis, Fresno, California.

(3) James AVENT, 9429 E. Harvey, Fresno, California,

(4) Howell GORDON, 9313 E. Lewis, Apt. A, Fresno, California.

(5) Buddy ALLEN, 9485 E. Tyler, Fresno, California.

At 10:00 A.M. Thomas and Junior HARKERSON, Howell GORDON and Fred AVENT were contacted at the HARKERSON residence where they were interviewed in the presence of Mrs. Harkerson. All denied any knowledge of the broken window.

Buddy ALLEN was contacted at his residence at approximately 11:00 A.M. and related the following:

At 10:00 P.M., 18 Aug. 61, he and the group mentioned above were en route home from the playground. As they approached the R & R COOLER COMPANY at 3884 North First Street, someone mentioned breaking a store window. Allen and Junior HARKERSON stated they wanted no part of it and continued walking. James AVENT, Howell GORDON, Thomas HARKERSON, and Boice MEYERS stopped in front of R & R COOLER COMPANY. ALLEN states that he and HARKERSON (Junior) had turned the corner at Lewis when they heard the sound of broken glass. Approximately 15 minutes later, the group met again at Lewis and Fisher Streets and the four suspects bragged, "Well, we broke the window."

All suspects, excepting James AVENT, were taken into custody at approximately 2:00 P.M. They were taken to the Fresno County Sheriff's Department and requestioned. MEYERS and Thomas HARKERSON admitted that they watched the incident, but stated they took no active part.

GORDON states James AVENT suggested that they break the window and while he was reaching for a rock, AVENT threw a piece of concrete against the window. It bounced back and AVENT supposedly threw again, smashing the window.

MEYERS' mother had previously disclosed that GORDON, presently on probation, had attempted to pawn his guitar to her on Sunday, 20 Aug. 61, in order to leave town. GORDON was booked at Juvenile Hall, Fresno, California. Thomas HARKERSON and Boice MEYERS were cited to the Juvenile Bureau.

James AVENT is visiting relatives in Southern California and is due back in approximately two weeks.

The victim requested restitution of $48.30 for the damage.

Case referred to Fresno County Sheriff's Department Juvenile Bureau for further action.

R. BAIN, Sgt. No. 10
23 Aug 61

IF ADDITIONAL SPACE IS REQUIRED USE CONT. REPORT, FORM 1-3

CASE	☐ UNFOUNDED	☐ D. A. DENIED COMPLAINT	INVESTIGATING OFFICER(S)
DECLARED	☐ BY ARREST	☐ COMPLAINT REFUSED	
CLOSED	☐ CONTINUED	BY VICTIM	BY Sgt. R. BAIN No. 10

OFFICE OF THE SHERIFF

JUVENILE INVESTIGATION REPORT

DATE & TIME OF THIS REPORT						CASE #	I.D. #
22 Aug 61 3:30PM						61-2573	

JUVENILE'S NAME (LAST, FIRST, MIDDLE)	ADDRESS	CITY	STATE	PHONE
GORDON, Howell Emory	9313 E. Lewis, Apt. A	Fresno	California	AM 9-1168

SEX	RACE	AGE	HEIGHT	WEIGHT	HAIR	EYES	COMPLEXION	BUILD	BIRTHDATE	BIRTHPLACE
M	W	16	5' 10½"	128	brn	ltbrn	ruddy	slend	20 Mar45	San Francisco

ALIAS OR NICKNAME	MARKS, SCARS, TATOOS, ETC.		DESCENT
"EMMY"	Acne scars about face		Irish-English

LAST SCHOOL ATTENDED	GRADE	RELIGION	YEARS IN CITY, COUNTY
Roosevelt High	10th	Prot.	12 years

FATHER'S NAME	ADDRESS	CITY	STATE	PHONE
Marvin Walter GORDON	unknown	Monterey	California	Unknown

MOTHER'S NAME	ADDRESS	CITY	STATE	PHONE
Martha RICE	9313 E. Lewis, Apt. A, Fresno		California	AM 7-4634

MARITAL STATUS (LIV. TOGETHER, DIV., SEP., ETC.)	IN LEGAL CUSTODY OF		ADDRESS	PHONE
Divorced	Mother		Same	Same

PROBATION STATUS (AT TIME OF ARREST)	CHARGE	PROBATION OFFICER	COUNTY OF	D.J.I. CHECKED. IF YES LIST RECORD BELOW) YES x NO
Probation	Theft	Mr. Spencer	Fresno	

OFFENSE	DATE-TIME OCCURRED	LOCATION OFFENSE COMMITTED	DATE AND TIME ARRESTED
700M W&I (Mal Misch)	18 Aug 61 10:PM	3884 N.First St., Fresno	22 Aug 61 3:PM

LOCATION OF ARREST	CONDITION AND ATTITUDE AT TIME OF ARREST	PARENT OR GUARDIAN NOTIFIED BY	DATE - TIME
Home	Poor	Sgt. R. Bain 22 Aug 61	

ARRESTING OFFICER'S DISPOSITION OF CASE	DATE	CITATION - APPEARANCE DATE AND TIME
Booked Juvenile Hall	22 Aug 61	3:PM

ADDITIONAL DETAILS:

SUBJECT was placed in Juvenile Hall, Fresno, after admitting he was involved in the breaking of a 70"x36" plate glass store window at approximately 10:00 P.M., 18 Aug. 61. The store window was located at 3884 North First Street, Fresno. The SUBJECT was involved along with Boice MEYERS (16), Thomas HARKERSON (13) and James AVENT (15). MEYERS and HARKERSON were cited to Juvenile Bureau 25 Aug. 61. AVENT is unavailable for contact as he is visiting relatives in Southern California and will be out of town for approximately two weeks.

It was found, during the investigation, that GORDON attempted to pawn his guitar Sunday, 20 Aug. 61, in order to get enough money to leave town.

Subject's attitude at the time of contact was very poor. He persisted in denying any knowledge of the broken window. His mother advises that she needs some assistance with this boy.

Damage to the window comes to $48.30 and victim desires restitution.

SEE: CRIME REPORT.
SEE: FOLLOW UP

IF ADDITIONAL SPACE IS REQUIRED USE CONT. REPORT, FORM 1-3

ARRESTING OFFICER	BADGE NO.	FOLLOW-UP	BADGE NO.	SUPERVISOR APPROVING	BADGE NO.
SGT. R. BAIN, No. 10		INVESTIGATOR			

OFFICE OF THE SHERIFF

DATE & TIME OF THIS REPORT	JUVENILE INVESTIGATION REPORT		CASE #	I. D. #
22 Aug 61 3:30 PM			61-2573	

JUVENILE'S NAME (LAST, FIRST, MIDDLE)			ADDRESS			CITY	STATE		PHONE
HARKERSON, Thomas Edward			9277 E. Lewis Street			Fresno	California		AM 4-3724

SEX	RACE	AGE	HEIGHT	WEIGHT	EYES	HAIR	COMPLEXION	BUILD	BIRTHDATE	BIRTHPLACE
M	W	13	4' 11"	110	Blue	brn	ruddy	small	6 Nov48	Fresno

ALIAS OR NICKNAME	MARKS, SCARS, TATOOS, ETC.		DESCENT
"TOMMY"	None		Norwegan-Irish

LAST SCHOOL ATTENDED		GRADE	RELIGION	YEARS IN CITY, COUNTY
Yosemite Jr. High		7th	Prot.	Life

FATHER'S NAME	ADDRESS	CITY	STATE	PHONE
Amos E. HARKERSON	Same Address			Same

MOTHER'S NAME	ADDRESS	CITY	STATE	PHONE
Mollie HARKERSON	Same Address			Same

MARITAL STATUS (LIV. TOGETHER, DIV., SEP., ETC.)	IN LEGAL CUSTODY OF	ADDRESS	PHONE
Living together	Parents		

PROBATION STATUS (AT TIME OF ARREST)	CHARGE	PROBATION OFFICER	COUNTY OF	C.I.I. CHECKED. (IF YES LIST RECORD BELOW) YES _X_ NO
States None				

OFFENSE	DATE-TIME OCCURRED	LOCATION OFFENSE COMMITTED	DATE AND TIME ARRESTED	
700M W&I (Mal Misch)	18 Aug 61 10:PM	3883 N.First St., Fresno	22 Aug 61	3:PM

LOCATION OF ARREST	CONDITION AND ATTITUDE AT TIME OF ARREST	PARENT OR GUARDIAN NOTIFIED BY	DATE -	TIME
Home	Poor	R.Bain, Sgt	22 Aug 61	3:PM

ARRESTING OFFICER'S DISPOSITION OF CASE	DATE	CITATION - APPEARANCE DATE AND TIME
Referred Juvenile Bureau		Cited 9:30 A.M. 25 Aug. 61

ADDITIONAL DETAILS:

SUBJECT was cited to Fresno County Sheriff's Department Juvenile Bureau after admitting involvement in the breaking of a 70" x 36" plate glass window at approximately 10:00 P.M., 18 Aug. 61. The store window was located at 3884 North First Street, Fresno. SUBJECT was involved with Boice MEYERS (16), Howell GORDON (16), and James AVENT (15). MEYERS was cited to the Juvenile Bureau for 10:00 A.M., 25 Aug. 61. GORDON was booked in the Juvenile Hall, Fresno, and AVENT was unavailable for contact as he is visiting in Southern California and will return in two weeks.

HARKERSON, at the time of first contact, was interviewed in the presence of his mother, and denied any knowledge of the broken window. Subject later admitted that he was in the group when the window was broken.

Damage amounts to $48.30 and victim desires restitution.

SEE: CRIME REPORT.

SEE: FOLLOW UP

IF ADDITIONAL SPACE IS REQUIRED USE CONT. REPORT, FORM 1-3

ARRESTING OFFICER	BADGE NO.	FOLLOW-UP	BADGE NO.	SUPERVISOR APPROVING	BADGE NO.
BY Sgt. R. BAIN No. 10		INVESTIGATOR			

OFFICE OF THE SHERIFF

DATE & TIME OF THIS REPORT	JUVENILE INVESTIGATION REPORT		CASE #	I. D. #
22 Aug 61 3:30PM			61-2573	

JUVENILE'S NAME (LAST, FIRST, MIDDLE)			ADDRESS			CITY		STATE		PHONE
MEYERS, Boice Eugene			9278 E. Lewis Street			Fresno		California		N/P

SEX	RACE	AGE	HEIGHT	WEIGHT	EYES	HAIR	COMPLEXION	BUILD	BIRTHDATE	BIRTHPLACE
M	W	16	5'7½"	145	blue	brn	ruddy	med	13 July 61	Delano

ALIAS OR NICKNAME	MARKS, SCARS, TATOOS, ETC.		DESCENT
"Punky"	TT "J" outer, lower left arm		Scotch-Irish

LAST SCHOOL ATTENDED	GRADE	RELIGION	YEARS IN CITY, COUNTY
Yosemite	8th	Prot.	1 Year

FATHER'S NAME	ADDRESS	CITY	STATE	PHONE
Leroy Paul MEYERS	9278 East Lewis Street	Fresno, Calif.		

MOTHER'S NAME	ADDRESS	CITY	STATE	PHONE
Pauline M. MEYERS	Same			

MARITAL STATUS (LIV. TOGETHER, DIV., SEP., ETC.)	IN LEGAL CUSTODY OF	ADDRESS	PHONE
Living together	Parents		

PROBATION STATUS (AT TIME OF ARREST)	CHARGE	PROBATION OFFICER	COUNTY OF	C.J.I. CHECKED, IF YES LIST RECORD BELOW YES_x_ NO
Probation	Run-Away	Mr. Spencer	Fresno	

OFFENSE	DATE-TIME OCCURRED	LOCATION OFFENSE COMMITTED	DATE AND TIME ARRESTED
700M W&I (Mal Misch)	18 Aug 61 10:PM	3884 N. First St., Fresno	22 Aug 61 3:PM

LOCATION OF ARREST	CONDITION AND ATTITUDE AT TIME OF ARREST	PARENT OR GUARDIAN NOTIFIED BY	DATE - TIME
At Home	Poor	Sgt. R. Bain	22 Aug 61 3:PM

ARRESTING OFFICER'S DISPOSITION OF CASE	DATE	CITATION - APPEARANCE DATE AND TIME
Referred Juvenile Bureau	22 Aug 61	Cited Juv. Bureau 10:AM 25 Aug 61

ADDITIONAL DETAILS:

Subject cited to Fresno County Sheriff's Department, Juvenile Bureau, after admitting he was involved in the breaking of a 70"x36" plate glass store window at approximately 10:00 P.M., 18 Aug. 61. The store window was located at 3884 North First Street, Fresno, California. Subject was involved along with Howell GORDON (16), Thomas HARKERSON (13) and James AVENT (15). HARKERSON cited to Juvenile Bureau 9:30 A.M., 25 Aug. 61. GORDON was booked in Juvenile Hall, Fresno, and AVENT was unavailable for contact since he is visiting in Southern California and is due back in two weeks.

MEYERS' attitude at time of contact was very poor. He denied any knowledge of the broken window and persisted in his attempt to cover up for GORDON and AVENT who actually threw the objects against the window.

Damages amount to $48.30 and victim desires restitution. . .

SEE: CRIME REPORT

SEE: FOLLOW-UP

IF ADDITIONAL SPACE IS REQUIRED USE CONT. REPORT, FORM 1-3

ARRESTING OFFICER	BADGE NO.	FOLLOW-UP	BADGE NO.	SUPERVISOR APPROVING	BADGE NO.
BY Sgt. R. BAIN	No. 10	INVESTIGATOR			

OFFICE OF THE SHERIFF

REPORTING DIVISION		FOLLOW UP REPORT	CASE NO.	
JUVENILE			61-2573	
CRIME CLASSIFICATION				DATE
P. C. 594				6 Sept. 61
NAME OF VICTIM		ADDRESS		PHONE
Charles TOORAM		9122 E. Kings Canyon, Fresno		AM 9-1168
	1 Howell GORDON (16)	ADDRESS 9313 E. Lewis Street, Fresno		PHONE AM 7-4634
SUSPECTS *	2 Thomas HARKERSON (13)	ADDRESS 9277 E. Lewis Street, Fresno		PHONE AM 4-3724
	3 Boice MEYERS (16)	ADDRESS 9278 E. Lewis Street, Fresno		PHONE N/P
	1 All suspects	ADDRESS		PHONE
PERSONS INTERVIEWED	2	ADDRESS		PHONE
	3	ADDRESS		PHONE
PERSONS ARRESTED				

* Susp. (4) James AVENT   (15) 9429 East Harvey, Fresno   AD 5-0442

SYNOPSIS: This report pertains to a Malicious Mischief (window smashed at a store building at 3884 North First Street, Fresno), and particularly pertains to interviews at the Juvenile Bureau and the final disposition of the case.

Suspects GORDON, HARKERSON and MEYERS appeared at the Juvenile Bureau at cited times, 25 Aug. 61. Both HARKERSON and MEYERS stated that on 18 Aug. 61, while in the company of GORDON and AVENT, the latter two suspects mentioned breaking a window. HARKERSON and MEYERS, not wanting to be involved, left the scene and after going around the corner, heard the sound of breaking glass. They were joined by GORDON and AVENT who stated they had just broken the window.

GORDON then was interviewed and admitted that he and AVENT stopped in front of the store where they both picked up chunks of cement. Each threw at the window simultaneously causing two fractures of the glass.

HARKERSON and MEYERS were reprimanded and released to their parents.

GORDON and his mother were advised of the name and address of the victim and of his right to restitution for his damages.

James AVENT and his parents appeared as per citation at 9:00 A.M. this date. AVENT readily admitted his part in the window smashing and implicated GORDON. Suspect AVENT and his parents were advised of the victim's right to collect for his damages and were requested to make restitution.

AVENT was then reprimanded and released to his parents.

The victim, Charles TOORAM, was phoned at 4:00 P.M. this date and advised of names and addresses of responsible parents. In the event restitution is not made as agreed, he may resort to a civil action.

CASE CLOSED.

SEE: CASE CLOSURE

SGT. R. BAIN   No. 10

IF ADDITIONAL SPACE IS REQUIRED USE CONT. REPORT, FORM 1-3

CASE	☐ UNFOUNDED	☐ D. A. DENIED COMPLAINT	INVESTIGATING OFFICER(S)
DECLARED	☐ BY ARREST	☐ COMPLAINT REFUSED	
CLOSED	☐ CONTINUED	BY VICTIM	BY Det. Flammang, Juvenile

OFFICE OF THE SHERIFF

DATE & TIME OF THIS REPORT	JUVENILE INVESTIGATION REPORT		CASE #	I.D. #
6 SEPT 61 9:30 AM			61-2573	

JUVENILE'S NAME (LAST, FIRST, MIDDLE)	ADDRESS	CITY	STATE	PHONE
AVENT, James William	9429 E. Harvey Avenue	Fresno	California	AD 5-0442

SEX	RACE	AGE	HEIGHT	WEIGHT	EYES	HAIR	COMPLEXION	BUILD	BIRTHDATE	BIRTHPLACE
M	W	15	5'6"	115	hzl	blde				

ALIAS OR NICKNAME	MARKS, SCARS, TATOOS, ETC.	DESCENT
"JIMMY"	1" Crescent cut scar outer right eyebrow	Irish-Indian

LAST SCHOOL ATTENDED	GRADE	RELIGION	YEARS IN CITY, COUNTY
Yosemite Jr. High School	9	Prot.	8 Years

FATHER'S NAME	ADDRESS	CITY	STATE	PHONE
G.T. AVENT	Same		Same	

MOTHER'S NAME	ADDRESS	CITY	STATE	PHONE
Irene A. AVENT	Same		Same	

MARITAL STATUS (LIV. TOGETHER, DIV., SEP., ETC.)	IN LEGAL CUSTODY OF	ADDRESS	PHONE
Living together	Parents		Same

PROBATION STATUS (AT TIME OF ARREST)	CHARGE	PROBATION OFFICER	COUNTY OF	D.J.I. CHECKED. IF YES LIST RECORD BELOW
Stated None				YES X NO

OFFENSE	DATE-TIME OCCURRED	LOCATION OFFENSE COMMITTED	DATE AND TIME ARRESTED
700M W&I (Mal Misd)	18 Aug 61 10:PM	3884 N. First St.,Fresno	6 Sept 61 9:AM

LOCATION OF ARREST	CONDITION AND ATTITUDE AT TIME OF ARREST	PARENT OR GUARDIAN NOTIFIED BY	DATE - TIME
Juvenile Bureau	Good	Flammang	6 Sept 61 9AM

ARRESTING OFFICER'S DISPOSITION OF CASE	DATE	CITATION - APPEARANCE DATE AND TIME
Reprimanded-Released to parents	6 Sept 61	6 Sept 61 9:AM

ADDITIONAL DETAILS:

SYNOPSIS: Subject involved in window smash on 18 Aug. 61. He was not handled until this date as he was in Los Angeles.

Subject appeared at the Juvenile Bureau with his parents at 9:00 A.M. on this date. AVENT readily admitted that he and Howell GORDON threw cement chunks at the store window, breaking same. His parents were then brought into the interview and he re-stated his admission.

AVENT'S statement cleared all suspects in this case, except himself and GORDON. His parents were advised that they would be jointly responsible with GORDON'S parents in making restitution of $48.30 to the victim in this case. The name and address of the victim were furnished to the AVENTS.

Subject was reprimanded and released to his parents.

SEE: FOLLOW-UP

11-9-61

IF ADDITIONAL SPACE IS REQUIRED USE CONT. REPORT, FORM 1-3

ARRESTING OFFICER	BADGE NO.	FOLLOW-UP	BADGE NO.	SUPERVISOR APPROVING	BADGE NO.
Det. Flammang	No. 107	INVESTIGATOR			

REFERENCE LIST

Handbooks (i.e., reference books for grammatical usage, punctuation, spelling, capitalization, form, and the like)

SUMNER IVES: *A New Handbook for Writers.* New York, Alfred A. Knopf, 1960.
> Contains all the usual handbook information, and in addition, a good structural sketch of English and sections on language and style.

ALBERT H. MARCKWARDT AND FREDERIC CASSIDY: *The Scribner Handbook of English.* New York, Charles Scribner's Sons, 1959.
> Deals with a number of usage problems related to grammar.

PORTER PERRIN AND GEORGE H. SMITH: *Handbook of Current English.* New York, Scott Foresman and Co., 1955.
> Contains complete sections on punctuation, spelling, capitalization, abbreviations, etc. Sections on grammar deal only with usage problems.

U. S. TREASURY DEPARTMENT, *Effective Revenue Writing, 1,* U.S. G.P.O., Training No. 82-0 (Rev. 5-61).
> Basic material designed to give brief and practical review of writing principles, grammar, and punctuation.

U. S. TREASURY DEPARTMENT, *Effective Revenue Writing, 2,* U.S. G.P.O., Training No. 129 (Rev. 7-62).
> Designed to help experienced writers and reviewers diagnose and cure writing weaknesses.

Grammars (contain information on usage as well)

DORA W. BROWN, WALLACE C. BROWN, AND DUDLEY BAILEY: *Form in Modern English.* New York, Oxford, 1958.

W. NELSON FRANCIS: *The Structure of American English.* New York, Ronald Press, 1958.

L. M. MYERS: *American English.* New York, Prentice Hall, 1952.

PAUL ROBERTS: *Understanding English.* New York, Harper and Brothers, 1958.

JAMES SLEDD: *A Short Introduction to English Grammar.* Chicago, Scott Foresman and Co., 1959.

Use of Words

S. I. HAYAKAWA: *Language in Thought and Action*. New York, Harcourt, Brace and Co., 1949 (rev. ed.).

Police Writing

JOHN C. HAZELET: *Police Report Writing*. Springfield, Thomas, 1960.

E. CAROLINE GABARD AND JOHN P. KENNEY: *Police Writing,* Springfield, Thomas, 1957.

INDEX

113